OUTDOOR
WOODWORKING

OUTDOOR
WOODWORKING
20 INSPIRING PROJECTS TO MAKE FROM SCRATCH

First published 2017 by
Guild of Master Craftsman Publications Ltd
Castle Place, 166 High Street, Lewes, East Sussex BN7 1XU, UK

ISBN 978 1 78494 247 2

All projects previously published in *Woodworking Plans & Projects* magazine, except for Adirondack Chair and Potting Bench.

A catalogue record for this book is available from the British Library.

Publisher: Jonathan Bailey
Production Manager: Jim Bulley
Editor: Alan Goodsell
Managing Art Editor: Gilda Pacitti
Designer: Ginny Zeal
Contributors: Anthony Bailey, Mark Baker, John Bee, Fred Byrne, Julie Byrne, Alan Goodsell, James Hatter, Alan Holtham, Jim Robinson, Simon Rodway, Andy Standing and Mike Whitewood
Photographers: All photographs by the project authors
Illustrator: Simon Rodway

Colour origination by GMC Reprographics
Printed and bound in Malaysia

A NOTE ON MEASUREMENTS
The imperial measurements in these projects have been converted from metric. While every attempt has been made to ensure they are accurate enough for practical purposes, some rounding up or down is inevitable. When following the projects always use metric or imperial measurements – never mix the two. If in doubt, make a full-sized working drawing before you begin.

Contents

Introduction

Here is a book that combines two of the world's favourite leisure activities: woodwork and gardening. Some of us divide the year into two seasons: the warmer months when the pleasantest place to be is in the garden, and the cooler, darker months when the workshop holds more attractions. The projects in this book are designed to help you get the best out of both workshop and garden all the year round.

The book begins and ends with two thoroughly practical garden items: the humble dibber and the ever-useful potting bench. In between, we have everything from simple planters to large-scale garden structures. The projects encompass every style from rustic to refined — one of our planters is based on the famous design used at the orangery at the palace of Versailles, no less. Some of the items are ruggedly built so they can be left outside in all weathers; others, like the elegant serving trolley, you will probably want to keep indoors when they are not being used.

Those of you who would rather spend time enjoying the garden than working in it will find many projects to your taste, from comfortable seating to an elegant lantern.

For many people, wildlife is an essential feature of the garden, so we have included a number of projects designed to encourage birds and bats to visit your garden.

Some projects are more elaborate than others, but none of them require exceptional woodworking skills, and the step-by-step instructions, accompanied by measured drawings and informative photographs, should make them accessible to everyone. Pick a project that's within your abilities, and take your time – woodwork and gardens are two pleasures that should never be rushed!

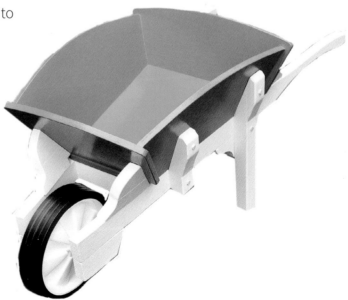

BIRD TABLE

John Bee builds the simplest of bird tables for the garden

My eldest son has just moved into a new house with a
large garden, which attracts many birds. With winter well
and truly established, his wife wants to make sure they
are well fed, so she asked me to make a rustic-looking bird
table for them and this was the result.

What you need

- 54in of 4 x 3in (1372mm of 100 x 75mm),
  54in of 4½ x 2½in (1372mm of 112 x 62mm)
  and 72in of 3 x 2in (1830mm of 75 x 50mm)
  rough-sawn timber
- Feather-edge boarding
- Barge boards
- Broom handle or dowel
- Tongue-and-groove boards

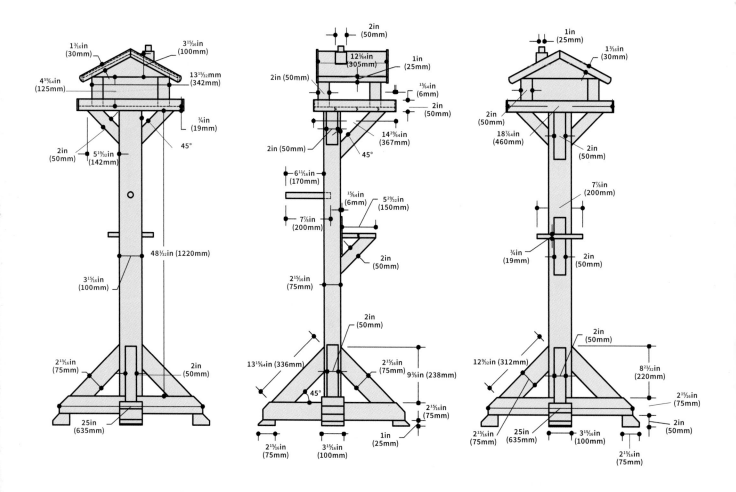

MAKING THE STAND

1-2 To make the stand, cut the 4 x 3in (100 x 75mm) wood to 48in (1220mm), then cut two pieces of the 4½ x 2½in (112 x 62mm) wood 25in (635mm) long and half lap joint them together. Cut a 45° chamfer off each end.

I made the half-lap joint with my sliding mitre saw, using the trenching facility. This could be cut with a tenon saw and a chisel or a router, either electrical or the old-fashioned type!

3-4 For ease of work, the top half of the base half joint must be fastened to the 4 x 3in (100 x 75mm) post upright first before the cross pieces are fastened together. Now cut four braces from the 3 x 2in (75 x 50mm) wood and chamfer the ends to 45°, then drill

screw holes and counterbore for decorative dowelling. Give the pieces a light sanding, then make two feet out of 4 x 2in (100 x 50mm) wood and two out of 4 x 1in (100 x 25mm), and again chamfer at 45°. Glue and screw them to the base cross pieces.

MAKING THE HOUSE

5-11 To make the little house, cut four pieces of 2 x 2in x 5in (50 x 50 x 125mm), two pieces of 4 x 1 x 13½in (100 x 25 x 342mm) and mark and cut the 2 x 2in (50 x 50mm) as shown in picture 6. For the roof I used a length of feather-edge boarding cut at 12in (305mm) long. On the 4 x 1in (100 x 25mm) pieces mark out the shape on the feather-edge board and again cut out. When fitting the roof panels to the glued and nailed end panels, glue and nail or screw the shaped 4 x 1in (100 x 25mm) front panel of the house to the 2 x 2in (50 x 50mm) supports. On the front of the house let the roof panels overhang by about 1in (25mm) or so, and make the back flush. For the barge board, front and back, I used a round architrave. Glue and screw it to the widest part of the roof panels.

12-13 To make the chimney, cut a piece of 3 x 2in (75 x 50mm) wood at 30° and cut to a length 3in (75mm) or so. For the chimney pots cut a piece of broom handle or 1in (25mm) dowel to 1in (25mm) long and glue and screw in position, then glue and screw the chimney assembly to the roof.

LANDING STRIP

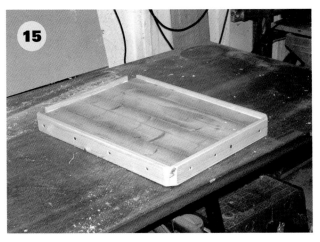

14-15 To make the table for the house to stand on and for the birds to land on I used tongue and groove cut to 18in (460mm) long and glued

and clamped together to a 14in (355mm) width. When cured, edge it all round with 2 x ¼in (50 x 6mm) strips glued and screwed on.

ATTACHING HOUSE TO BASE

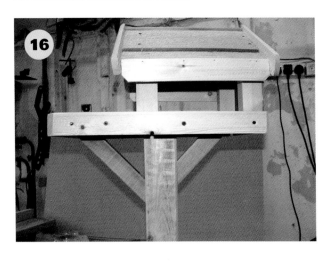

16-17 Screw the base onto the upright post and brace it with 2 x 2in (50 x 50mm) braces, again cut at 45° and fastened to post and base. Position

the house to the rear of the base to provide a platform for the birds to land on and a place for their feed.

FINISHING TOUCHES

18-19 I decided to cover the screw heads with plugs to match the studs on the stand braces, gluing them over and touching up with stain.

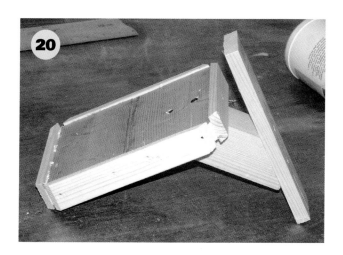

20 The small feeding tray is made from tongue-and-groove offcuts, measures 8 x 6in (200 x 150mm) and is chamfered at 45°. A piece of 2 x ¼in (50 x 6mm) wood is glued and screwed to one end so it can be fastened to the centre post. Around the back I let in an 8in (200mm)-long piece of 1in (25mm) dowel to serve as a perch and something on which to fasten nets of nuts and seeds.

21 This table is so sturdy that I'd be ready to bet it could take the weight of an eagle, and it certainly won't blow over in the wind.

Tip

It is easier to stain the house before fastening to the base. Staining the stand is also easier because it can be put on the base to stain the underside.

WINDOW BOX

Mark Baker's finger-jointed window box is built from waterproof exterior ply

What you need

- ½in (12mm) exterior ply
- Jigsaw/handsaw
- Hammer
- Chisel
- Drill
- Masonry bit

- ⅜–½in (10–12mm) drill bit
- Wall plugs
- Screws
- Waterproof adhesive
- Abrasive down to 320 grit
- Appropriate external finish

- Ruler
- Pencil
- Square
- Protractor
- Webbing straps/clamps
- Spirit level

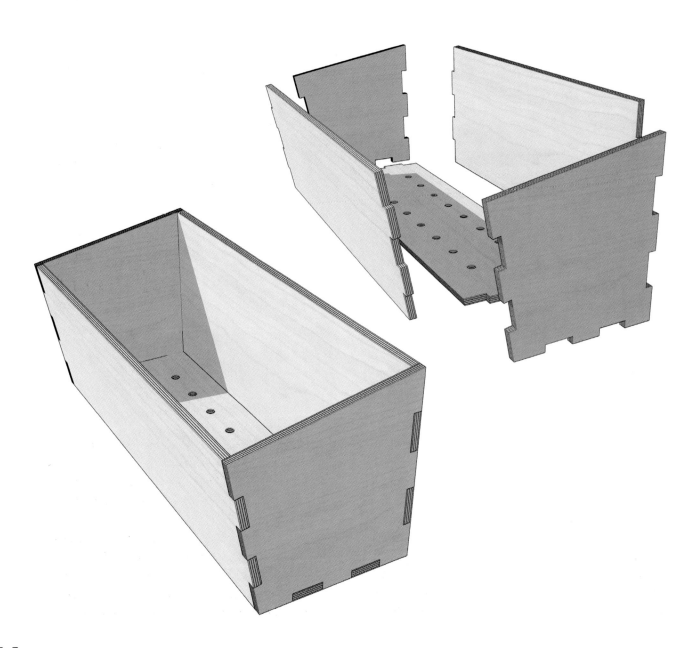

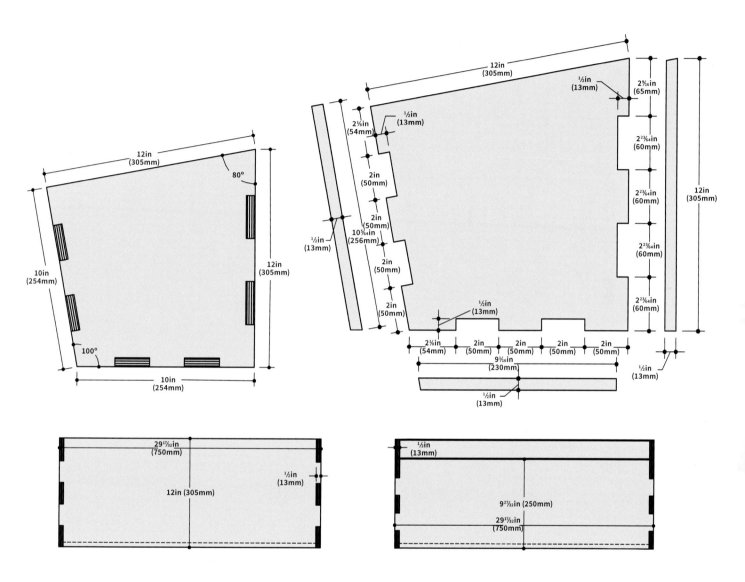

HOW TO MAKE IT

Cut the bottom, sides, front and back to overall dimensions, then use a protractor or scribing method on the two ends to create the slope from front to back, and from bottom to leading edge. Use a jigsaw or handsaw to cut the marked finger-joint positions. Clean up the corners with a hammer and chisel, then try for a test fit. Drill the drainage holes in the bottom panel. Glue up the joints with waterproof adhesive, then bring everything together and use either webbing straps or clamps to hold the pieces in place until the glue is set. For extra strength –

though not strictly necessary – fit a length of wood across the bottom front and rear edges and screw the front lower edge and lower back and back panel to the relevant components. Sand the window box to a fine finish then apply an exterior finish.

Drill three equally spaced holes along the back panel. Position the box under windowsill and mark the hole positions, ensuring the box is level. Drill and fit wall plugs and screw the window box into position. Fill the window box with soil and plant out with flowers or vegetables.

PATIO DINER

Anthony Bailey puts together a nifty set for those warm summer nights

There is plenty of outdoor furniture on the market, but this design is more compact than most and is made from hardwood for a longer life and nicer appearance than softwood. It can be made in a two- or four-seat version and the construction is relatively simple and straightforward. Oak weathers to a silvery grey with age and needs little maintenance although it is better, as with any wood, if it is on a hardstanding such as a patio to avoid rot.

What you need

- MDF and wood/material of choice
- Planer/thicknesser
- Bandsaw
- Power sander
- Biscuit jointer or router with biscuit cutter
- Chamfer bit
- G-clamps
- Sash cramps
- Wood glue and brushes
- Edge-jointing jig
- Gloss lacquer
- 100-grit wet and dry paper
- Wood primer
- Oil-based eggshell paint

Cutting list

TABLE TOP SLATS	2 @ $35\frac{7}{16}$ x $4\frac{59}{64}$ x 1in (900 x 125 x 25mm)		TABLE TOP BRACES	2 @ $33\frac{5}{64}$ x $1\frac{49}{64}$ x 1in (840 x 45 x 25mm)
TABLE TOP SLATS	2 @ $32\frac{7}{8}$ x $4\frac{59}{64}$ x 1in (835 x 125 x 25mm)		SEAT BRACES	4 @ $7\frac{3}{32}$ x $1\frac{49}{64}$ x 1in (180 x 45 x 25mm)
TABLE TOP SLATS	2 @ $24\frac{39}{64}$ x $4\frac{59}{64}$ x 1in (625 x 125 x 25mm)		SEAT SUPPORTS	2 @ $70\frac{55}{64}$ x $1\frac{49}{64}$ x 1in (1800 x 45 x 25mm)
SEAT SLATS	4 @ $13\frac{25}{32}$ x $6\frac{11}{64}$ x 1in (350 x 160 x 25mm)		ANGLED LEGS	2 @ $36\frac{13}{16}$ x $2\frac{9}{16}$ x $1\frac{27}{64}$in (935 x 65 x 36mm)
TABLE TOP BRACES	2 @ $20\frac{55}{64}$ x $1\frac{49}{64}$ x 1in (530 x 45 x 25mm)		LEGS	2 @ $27\frac{23}{64}$ x $2\frac{31}{64}$ x 2in (695 x 63 x 50mm)
TABLE TOP BRACES	2 @ x $29\frac{59}{64}$ x $1\frac{49}{64}$ x 1in (760 x 45 x 25mm)		LEG BRACES	2 @ $29\frac{1}{16}$ x $1\frac{49}{64}$ x 1in (738 x 45 x 25mm)

PREPARATION

1 Leave the sections overlength as there are various shapes that need marking out and cutting with a jigsaw or bandsaw later on. Make sure you avoid any defects when selecting the timber, as these areas will be more vulnerable to weather than sound wood. As usual, plane the face and edge of each component overhand, checking the surfaces are flat and true to each other when checked with a square. Although it may seem

that this isn't quite so critical on a rustic project, it is much easier to get your initial preparation done properly if you have been careful with setting out.

2 Once all overhanding is done, set up for thicknessing. Machine the edges first while the boards are thick enough to run through, so they sit squarely on the thicknesser bed. Now thickness your wood.

MAKING THE TABLE TOP

The table, which can be varied in size to suit your situation, is the heart of the project. There are two obvious ways to go about shaping it. The first is to draw out a full-size template using a long trammel consisting of a wooden bar, a pencil fixed at one end and a nail or screw at the other end for the rotation point.

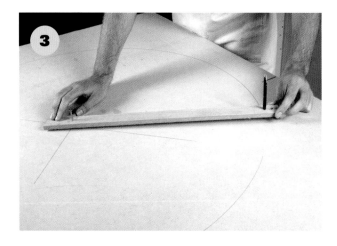

3 Lay each piece out and mark out the shape again using the trammel.

4 The completed template.

5 The second method is to screw the overlength sections to the cross-members that go underneath so it all becomes a solid unit. Note that the halving joints need to be cut in these members first. Now place it across trestles and use a powerful jigsaw set on full orbital action to cut a line.

6 Then take each piece to the bandsaw and cut the curved ends to the pencil line. Remember to mark the pieces first so you reassemble them in the right order.

Patterned top

A–B To be a bit different, a lazy diamond pattern can be machined into the top using a router and a V-point cutter. It looks good, but also has the benefit of aiding water run-off. You can do this by clamping a wooden bar as a fence on the top after drawing out the complete diamond pattern.

7–9 In each case, once the top is fully assembled, stand it on edge and do some deft belt sanding around the perimeter to get a smooth and regular curve.

FIXINGS

The table and seat slats can be screwed to the underneath members with weather-resistant decking screws, whereas those members where they cross over or join other components need to be bolted together, preferably using galvanized or coated bolts and nylon locknuts of the correct length. A cordless drill and the correct deck screwdriver bit, plus drill bits for pre-drilling the tough oak, are required.

LEGS TO FRAME

10–11 The angled legs are marked out using the angles shown on the drawing as a guide: use a compound mitre saw for a clean-cut finish. Bolt them to the members under the top and to the members that support the seats.

12 You should now have a solid if unstable structure due to the lack of the two upright legs. The upright legs are halved to sit halfway over the crosswise members that sit under the top. There are also lower frame members that make the legs solid once bolted together.

SEATS

13 The seats are simple round shapes, so you sit astride them with the angled leg in front of you. Again, mark out with a trammel allowing a suitable gap between the two components. Now screw them firmly to the two supporting members using deck screws.

SANDING AND FINISHING

14 The general sanding was of course done early on, but edges and ends of all components need attention with abrasive paper to make them safe and comfortable as oak can shed large splinters on very square edges. Strictly speaking oak can be left bare, exposed to the elements. However, Danish oil or decking oil will help to improve the survival properties of the wood. It should be re-applied every year.

Alternative four-seater

In this case four sets of angled legs and four seats are required. The extra ones are added in exactly the same way as the first two legs and seats. However, the cross members fit underneath the existing cross members, making the seats lower, and they feature smaller seats, thus making them perfect for children!

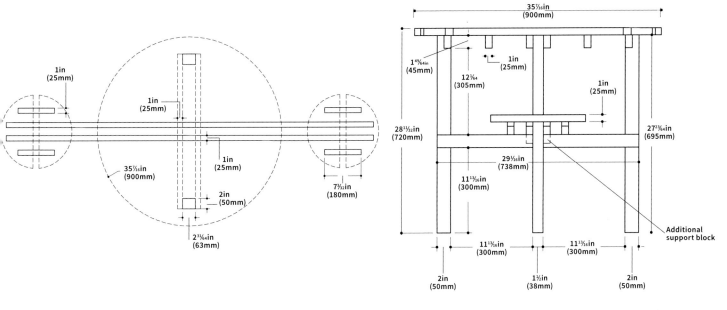

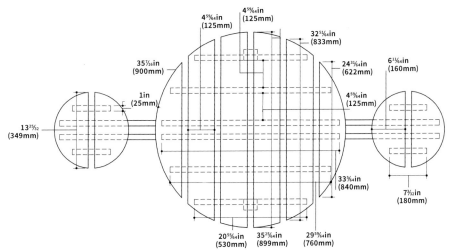

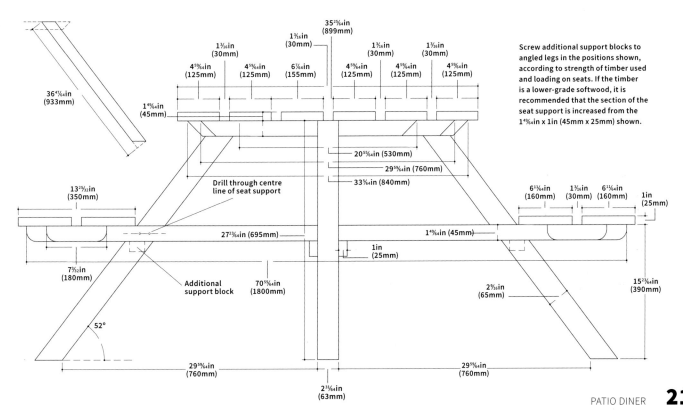

Screw additional support blocks to angled legs in the positions shown, according to strength of timber used and loading on seats. If the timber is a lower-grade softwood, it is recommended that the section of the seat support is increased from the 1⁴⁹⁄₆₄in x 1in (45mm x 25mm) shown.

TEALIGHT LANTERN

Julie Byrne lights up your garden with a charming tealight project

What you need

- Scrollsaw fitted with a no.5 blade
- ³⁄₁₆ & ¼in (4 & 6mm) birch plywood
- Drill with ¹⁄₁₆ & ¼in (1.5 & 6mm) drill bits
- Masking tape
- 180–240 sandpaper
- PVA/white glue
- Coloured acrylic sheets/90g tracing paper
- Scissors
- Clamps or large elastic bands
- 4 screw eyes
- Length of fine chain
- Finish of choice

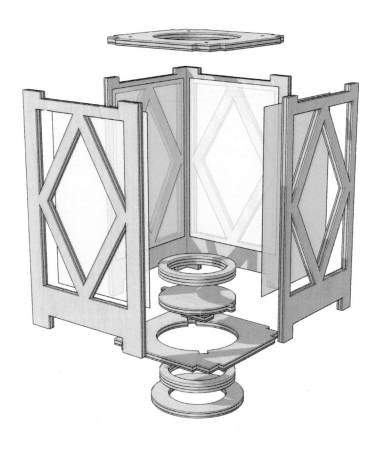

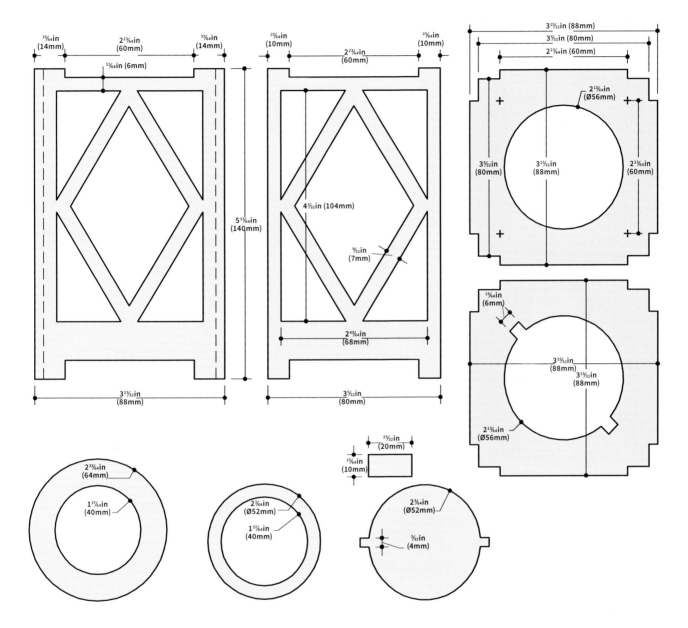

HOW TO MAKE IT

First cut four pieces 5½ x 3½in (140 x 88mm) from the ³⁄₁₆in (4mm) plywood. These side panels can then be stacked together with masking tape and be cut as one, as can the two circles using the ¼in (6mm) ply.

Transfer the patterns onto the prepared pieces and drill the blade entry holes for the inner cuts, then continue to cut out all the pieces.

Separate the four side panels into two pairs and re-tape if necessary, then, still referring to the pattern, trim off the ³⁄₁₆in (4mm) strip along each side of two of the pieces. Drill the four pilot holes in the top section using the ¹⁄₁₆in (1.5mm drill) bit and lightly sand all the pieces, then remove any dust. Next adhere the coloured acrylic sheets or if wished the slightly opaque tracing paper to the inside of each panel.

Glue and secure together the side panels and the top and bottom sections, then glue in order the five circular pieces that make up the bayonet section and allow the glue to dry. All that's left to do is apply a finish of your choice and when dry attach the four screw eyes and chain.

GARDEN GATE

Anthony Bailey's gate needs a fair amount of technique, but will yield excellent results

The choice of timber is important because of weathering and rot. The baseline choice is European redwood, which needs regular treatment to reduce the onset of decay and to keep it looking good. This can have an oil or paint finish, but not a microporous type.

Next is Siberian larch which, without any ground contact (where decay starts due to bacteria in the soil), has a huge lifespan, although in realistic terms is generally much shorter due to the environment it is situated in.

Then there are African hardwoods – specifically Idigbo and Meranti – both species have longevity and look good too. Maintenance is reduced with these woods but of course they cost more.

A key feature is having posts properly set in the ground in concrete to a decent depth: usually about 30in (760mm) minimum especially for the double driveway gates, which add more strain on the posts.

Another vital feature, apart from the wedged mortise and tenons, are the bracings on the reverse of each gate. These stop them from eventually sagging out of shape.

What you need
- Choice of hard and softwoods, per cutting list
- ½in (13mm) collet capacity router and long straight cutter
- Biscuit cutter
- Hammer
- Mitre saw
- Wood finish of choice

Cutting list

Double Gate

POSTS	2 @ $66\frac{5}{64}$ x $3\frac{47}{64}$ x $3\frac{47}{64}$ in (1700 x 95 x 95mm)
STILES	4 @ $32\frac{3}{32}$ x $2\frac{3}{4}$ x $2\frac{11}{64}$ in (815 x 70 x 55mm)
TOP RAILS	2 @ $48\frac{1}{2}$ x $3\frac{47}{64}$ x $1\frac{49}{64}$ in (1220 x 95 x 45mm)
MID RAILS	2 @ $48\frac{1}{2}$ x $3\frac{47}{64}$ x $1\frac{49}{64}$ in (1220 x 95 x 45mm)
BOTTOM RAILS	2 @ $48\frac{1}{2}$ x $3\frac{47}{64}$ x $1\frac{49}{64}$ in (1220 x 95 x 45mm)
BRACES	4 @ $23\frac{55}{64}$ x $2\frac{3}{4}$ x $2\frac{9}{32}$ in (606 x 70 x 23mm)
LONG SLATS	4 @ $10\frac{3}{64}$ x $2\frac{3}{4}$ x $5\frac{5}{64}$ in (255 x 70 x 22mm)
SHORT SLATS	4 @ $8\frac{27}{64}$ x $2\frac{3}{4}$ x $5\frac{5}{64}$ in (214 x 70 x 22mm)
VERTICAL BOARDS	15 @ $12\frac{13}{64}$ x $5\frac{45}{64}$ x $5\frac{5}{64}$ in (310 x 145 x 22mm)
WEDGES	24 @ to fit

Cutting list

Single Gate

POSTS	2 @ $66\frac{5}{64}$ x $3\frac{47}{64}$ x $3\frac{47}{64}$ in (1700 x 95 x 95mm)
STILES	2 @ $37\frac{19}{32}$ x $2\frac{3}{4}$ x $2\frac{11}{64}$ in (955 x 70 x 55mm)
TOP RAIL	1 @ $36\frac{7}{32}$ x $5\frac{33}{64}$ x $1\frac{49}{64}$ in (920 x ex140 x 45mm)
MID RAIL	1 @ $36\frac{7}{32}$ x $5\frac{33}{64}$ x $1\frac{49}{64}$ in (920 x 95 x 45mm)
BOTTOM RAIL	1 @ $36\frac{7}{32}$ x $5\frac{33}{64}$ x $1\frac{49}{64}$ in (920 x 95 x 45mm)
BRACE	1 @ $33\frac{55}{64}$ x $2\frac{3}{4}$ x $2\frac{9}{32}$ in (860 x 70 x 23mm)
LONG SLATS	2 @ $10\frac{15}{32}$ x $2\frac{3}{4}$ x $5\frac{5}{64}$ in (266 x 70 x 22mm)
SHORT SLAT	1 @ $8\frac{1}{2}$ x $2\frac{3}{4}$ x $5\frac{5}{64}$ in (216 x 70 x 22mm)
VERTICAL BOARD	6 @ $15\frac{13}{64}$ x $5\frac{45}{64}$ x $5\frac{5}{64}$ in (386 x 145 x 22mm)
WEDGES	12 @ to fit

PREPARATION

1–2 Following the cutting list, saw and plane all components, leaving them overlength. The version described here is constructed from meranti, which we found in readily usable prepared sections so there wasn't much planing required. Since meranti isn't normally available as tongue and groove to clad the fronts of these gates, we chose a type of hardwood decking referred to as 'thermowood', which has a long lifespan but is thicker than tongue-and-groove boards.

MAKING THE STILES

Mark out the mortises, offsetting towards the front, so all components will be flush on the front face; also mark the small curve at the top and bandsaw it out. To machine the mortises without the advantage of a chisel mortiser, you will need a ½in (13mm) collet-capacity router and a long straight cutter and two side fences. Hold the stile in the vice and sit the router on it, and set for the maximum cut depth possible. If the cutter won't reach right through, you can turn the stile over and machine from the other side. Move the fences in so as to clamp the router firmly on the stile, set the cutter to one side of the mortise, and machine gradually to depth.

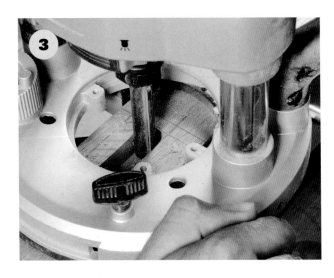

3 Then move it over and do the other side of the mortise, repeating from the other side as previously described. Note that the tenons are wedged on the outside of the stile, so chisel cut a slope from the outside at both ends of the mortise. Repeat with the other two mortises.

THE TOP RAIL

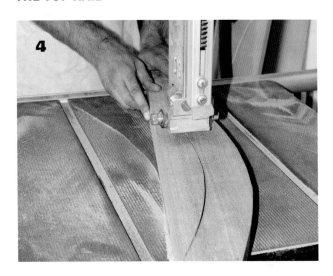

4 Mark out the curves on the top rail then bandsaw and belt sand to shape.

5 Now mark the tenons and bandsaw these out including the shoulders.

MID AND BOTTOM RAILS

The bottom rail can be deeper than the mid rail but the treatment of both is the same.

6 A largish rebate is needed to accommodate the cladding.

7 Each end will need a tenon cut on the bandsaw.

8 A vital point is to cut out the recesses for the bracing. However it is better to dry assemble the gates first and then mark where these should be before cutting.

MAKING THE SLATS

9 These fit between the upper and mid rails. Mark out the mortise positions and machine them out using the router as before. However, the underside of the rail is curved so only the centre mortise can be accurately done like this. The outer ones are probably better done using chain drilling in which a line of drill holes which are then made into one slot using a sharp chisel. The slats are 'barefaced' tenons in effect, so they need to be a neat tidy fit. The curved edges match the holes and are machined on the router table.

DRY ASSEMBLY

10 After a trial fit to make sure it all goes together properly, mark for the bracing, cut out the brace pieces and check the fit.

11 Cut the slats to length and check the fit again.

12-15 Now reassemble as before but this time your gate or gates won't be coming apart again. Cabinetmakers kerf the tenons and drive wedges into the kerfs. However, as this is joinery, a joiner's method is to drive the wedges down either side of the

tenon, which is what we will do. The tenons should be slightly overlength as are the wedges. Trim them off flush once assembly is complete. Cut and fit the cladding into the rebates in the rails and pin in place.

16 Quickly sand over and apply a suitable finish.

17 The remaining task is to hang the gates using suitable hardware and fit a latch, or a flip-over gate-closer in the case of the driveway version.

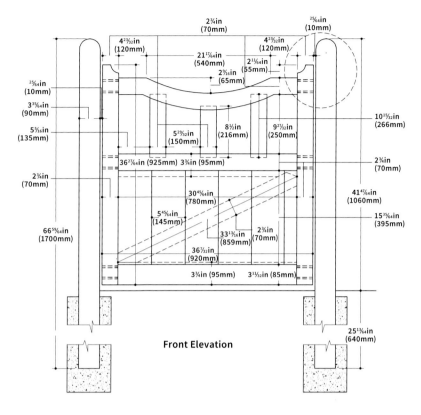

Front Elevation

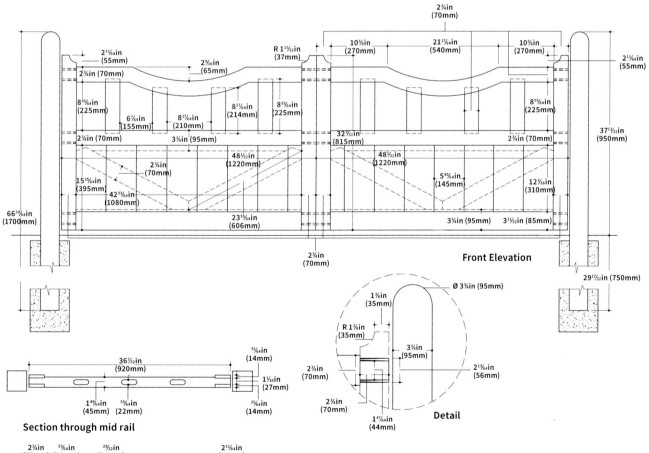

Front Elevation

Section through mid rail

Section through vertical boarding and brace

Detail

VERSAILLES PLANTER

Mark Baker and Anthony Bailey use old pallets to create this attractive garden planter

If you have a day to spare and want to create an ideal garden planter that will cost you nothing but some paint, a few screws and a bit of elbow grease, why not give this project a try? Acquiring the pallets should be relatively easy as many companies pay to have them taken away. So you can boost your green credentials by recycling while you create this elegant planter inspired by those designed for the gardens of Versailles near Paris in the 17th century.

Cutting list

LEGS	12 @ 24¾ x 2¾ x (ex)1in (630 x 70 x (ex)25mm)
TOP/BOTTOM RAILS	8 @ 21½ x 2¾ x 1in (540 x 70 x 25mm)
VERTICAL BOARD	To fit 2 sides 18 x 19⁵⁄₁₆ x 1in (460 x 490 x 25mm)
VERTICAL BOARD	To fit 2 sides 17⅛ x 19⁵⁄₁₆ x 1in (435 x 490 x 25mm)
TOP FIXING BATTEN	2 @ 19⁵⁄₁₆ x 1⅝ x ¹¹⁄₁₆in (490 x 40 x 17mm)
BOTTOM FIXING BATTEN	2 @ 19⁵⁄₁₆ x 1⅛ x 1in (490 x 30 x 25mm)
BOTTOM SLATS	1 @ 21½ x 1⅛ x 1in (540 x 30 x 25mm)

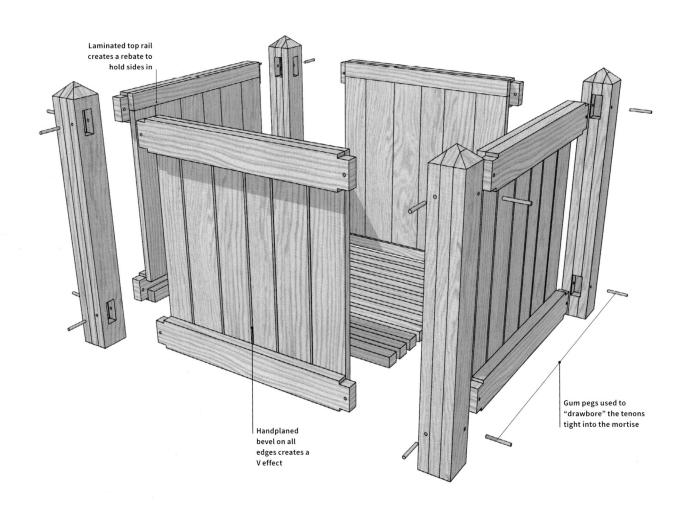

Laminated top rail creates a rebate to hold sides in

Handplaned bevel on all edges creates a V effect

Gum pegs used to "drawbore" the tenons tight into the mortise

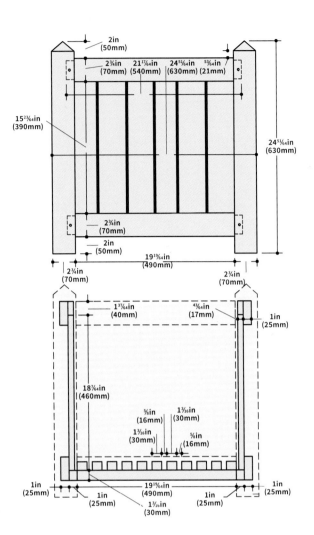

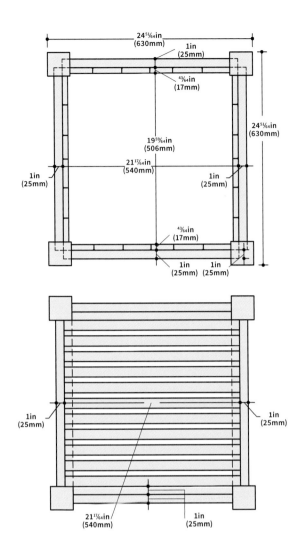

Finding the pallets

Step one is to locate some pallets. These can be obtained from companies who have deliveries. Many have to pay to dispose of the pallets so we were pleasantly surprised that when we asked if we could have some we were told we could have as many as we wanted. The pallets came in both hardwood and softwood versions. We have used softwood pallets for this project and took six in all. We have used the wood as supplied and left the 'sawn' effect from the salvaged boards to create a rustic texture on the planter.

Take apart the pallets. To save time, using a circular saw, we cut the boards through the ends of the pallets on the inside face of the end blocks then the rest could be taken apart with a claw hammer and block to leave the long middle sections intact. The board thicknesses may vary slightly but do not worry about this, this small discrepancy will not show.

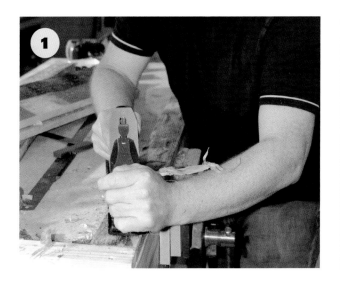

1 Four corner uprights are required and since we are working with boards, the best way to create the uprights is to laminate them. Take three boards and cut them to 24¾in (630mm) length and 2¾in (70mm) width. The reason for 2¾in (70mm) is that the boards are each about ⅞in (23mm) thick so once the three boards were placed together this made a square(ish) upright. Since we need to laminate then, plane the meeting faces to ensure a good fit, then glue (using waterproof glue).

2 Clamp the faces together, then screw them together – a failsafe device should the glue fail.

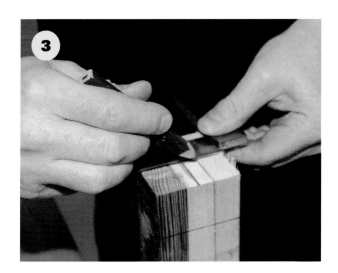

3 I wanted a classical appearance so decided to mark and cut a traditional point on the top of the uprights. Mark 1in (25mm) down from the end and square this line around. Then mark the centre of the upright on the top and draw a line to meet the side marking to the centre. This will create the point, then cut it by hand or on a bandsaw.

4 Once cut, take the sharp corners off each upright with a plane.

CROSS RAILS

5 Now take eight boards and cut them to 22in (560mm) length and 2¾in (70mm) width. These will form the top and bottom rails. At each end mark a bare-faced shouldered tenon. The shoulders are ½in (13mm) deep and the tenon is 1⅜in (35mm) long. The shoulders will ensure a nice clean fit against the uprights. The end of the tenon needs to be mitred so it fits nicely against the other cross rail, which will meet it in the middle of the upright.

6 Once all the tenons are cut you need to mark the uprights for the positions of the mortises – the holes in which the tenons fit. Measure 1½in (38mm) down from the bottom shoulder of the point you have just cut, then lay the tenon up against this mark and mark the width of

the tenon on the upright. This will be the mortise hole size to be cut. The shoulders on the tenon are ½in (13mm) so when the mortise is cut and all is clamped tight the top of the rail will sit 1in (25mm) below the shoulder of the point on the top of the upright.

Continue this on the other four uprights until all 8 mortise hole positions have been mark for the top rails. Now measure 2½in (63mm) from the bottom of the uprights and mark the mortise positions as before for the bottom rails too. This will mean that the bottom of the rail will sit 2in (50mm) off the floor. Note that since this is a single board, it is the same width as the middle lamination of the upright.

7 Now cut the mortises and then dry fit and clamp all the components together to make sure everything fits together.

8 Once happy that everything fits snugly and is square and so on, glue and clamp all the side rails and uprights together. As a safety aspect, drill a ¼in (6mm) hole in the side of the upright to pass straight through the tenon and insert a ¼in (6mm) dowel. This will act as a locking device should the glue fail.

INSIDE FACE OF THE RAILS AND BOTTOM

9 The next phase is to cut and screw four lengths of wood 1⅛ x 1⅛in (30 x 30mm) or so square x 19⁵⁄₁₆in (490mm) long around the bottom edge of the lower rails so the bottom of the wood is flush with the bottom edge of the lower rails. We found a pallet with a thicker board size in it, but ⅞in (23mm) square is fine. Then cut four pieces 19⁵⁄₁₆in (490mm) long by 1⅝in (40mm) deep and ⅞in (23mm) thick (or the thickness of board) and screw these to the top rails so that the top of these pieces are flush with the top edge of the rails. Then cut 11 strips of wood about 1⅛ x 1⅛in (30 x 30mm), or whatever the square is of the pallet boards you are using, and screw these equidistantly along the bottom of the planter.

FINISHING

SIDES

10 Now measure and fit the panels in the sides. These boards are full pallet width sizes and vary in width somewhat: just measure them out and cut what is necessary to make the boards fit. Once cut to size, screw them in place. Note that the boards are supported so that if you fill the planter with earth (a membrane will have to be placed on the bottom to prevent the soil from falling through the slats) the pressure will not force the boards off the face off the planter. Everything is supported behind the rails.

11 All that remains is to treat the planter with a preservative, let it dry and paint with an exterior fence or panel paint of your choice. I suppose you could undercoat it and apply a top coat of your choice if you desire but I chose a panel paint that contrasts well with the cordyline planted in it and the stones on which it was to sit. There you have it: a planter in a day and one that is inexpensive to make.

PATIO TROLLEY

Mike Whitewood has come up with a wonderful way to make catering for summer barbecues more streamlined.

I don't know what it's like at your place but, at mine, there never seems to be enough space for things when we're dining al fresco. We always seem to need to run a shuttle service to bring stuff from the house, and then take other stuff back because there's nowhere outside to put it. This patio trolley is built from sapele and iroko, can be easily moved around and has a removable top tray.

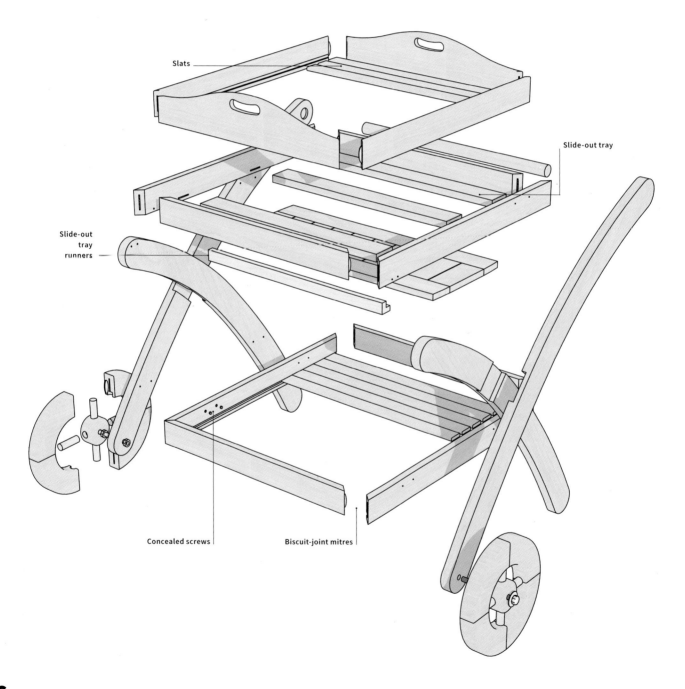

Slats

Slide-out tray

Slide-out tray runners

Concealed screws

Biscuit-joint mitres

Cutting list

LEGS	2 @ Ex 47¼ x 3 15/16 x 1in approx (Ex 1200 x 100 x 25mm approx)
LEGS	2 @ Ex 38½ x 3 15/16 x 1in approx (Ex 980 x 100 x 25mm approx)
WHEELS	8 @ Ex 5 29/32 x 5 29/32 x 1½in approx (Ex 150 x 150 x 38mm approx)
HUB	2 @ Ex 3 5/32 x 3 5/32 x 1½in approx (Ex 80 x 80 x 38mm approx)
DOWELS	8 @ 2 33/64 x ¾in diameter (64 x 19mm diameter)
HANDLE	1 @ 24 31/64 x 1in diameter (622 x 25mm diameter)

Bottom Tray

SIDES	2 @ 28 7/64 x 2 33/64 x ¾in (714 x 64 x 19mm)
ENDS	2 @ 23½ x 2 33/64 x ¾in (597 x 64 x 19mm)
SLATS	14 @ 22 41/64 x 1½ x 25/64in (575 x 38 x 10mm)

Upper Tray

SIDES	2 @ 28 7/64 x 2 33/64 x ¾in (714 x 64 x 19mm)
ENDS	2 @ 23½ x 2 33/64 x ¾in (597 x 64 x 19mm)
BEARERS	3 @ 22 x 2 33/64 x ¾in (559 x 64 x 19mm)

Lift-out Tray

SIDES	2 @ 26 11/16 x 2 33/64 x 33/64in (678 x 64 x 13mm)
ENDS	2 @ 22 x 4 31/64 x 33/64in (559 x 114 x 13mm)
SLATS	14 @ 21⅜ x 1½ x 25/64in (543 x 38 x 10mm)

Slide-out Tray

SIDES	2 @ 25 35/64 x 2 33/64 x ⅝in (649 x 64 x 16mm)
SLATS	10 @ 5 33/64 x 2 33/64 x ⅝in (140 x 64 x 16mm)
BEARERS	2 @ Ex 22 x 1½ x 1 17/64in (Ex 559 x 38 x 32mm)

PREPARATION

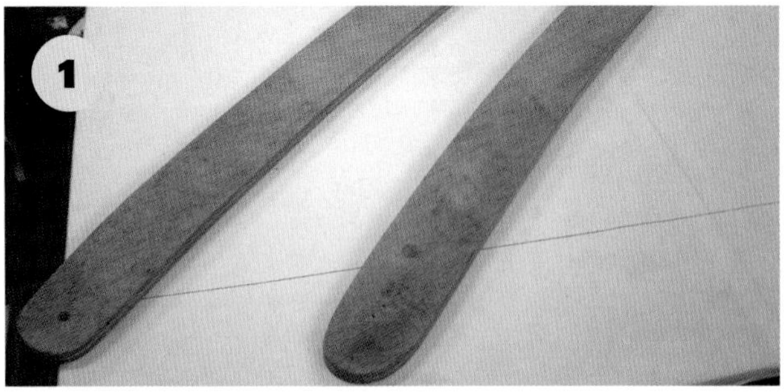

1 The first thing I did was to make a full-size drawing of the trolley on a piece of ¾in (19mm) ply. I began by marking the overall length and height of the trolley and drawing a rectangle, using the bottom edge of the plywood to represent the ground, ensuring that the trays would be parallel to it. Next, I drew the wheels using a large pair of compasses. The centre points of these are important as they mark the position of the axle and the handle and guide construction of the X-frame members. Once everything was marked out as per the plans, the next job was to prepare the stock using the radial-arm saw, jointer, tablesaw and thicknesser.

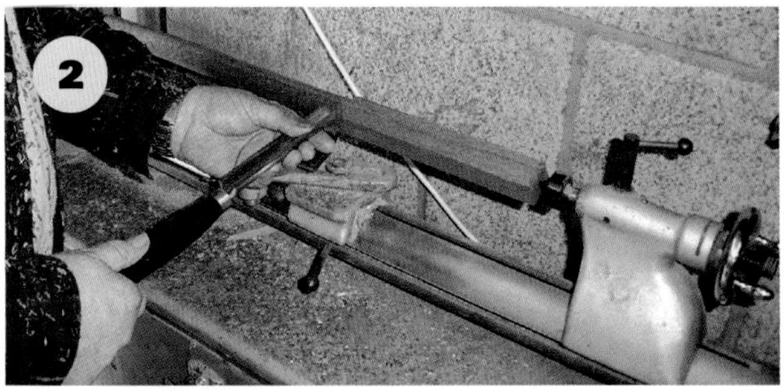

2 Once the blanks were prepped, I marked out the X-frames using the templates and rough cut them at the bandsaw. I then secured the templates to one pair of blanks. The long template was secured to the blank with ¾in (19mm) screws, and a single brad in the middle. The short one was secured with a couple of brads. Ensure the templates are fixed to what will be the inside faces of the members. The screw holes will be used when drilling the holes for the axle and handle. The blanks were then trimmed at the router table using a long bearing-guided straight bit and guide pin. I repeated the process on the other two blanks, flipping the templates to give mirror image sets.

MARKING OUT THE X-FRAMES

3 This operation was quite challenging because it involved cutting a halving joint, but there are no straight lines so normal marking out was not possible, although a marking gauge was used. I started by placing both long members on the rod and, using a small combination square, marked the intersection.

4 The short members were marked in the same way. I next placed one on top of the other, lining up the marks just made, and marked the position of each member on the other. It is essential at this stage to mark the waste areas to ensure that the frames are mirror images. I used the marking gauge to mark the centres.

SAWING THE X-FRAMES

5 Before cutting the joint I drilled the holes for the axle and handle while the parts were easier to manage, making sure that the axle counterbore was on the outside face and the handle hole in the inner face.

6 There are a number of ways to cut the halving joints and I opted for removing the majority of waste with the radial-arm saw. I set the saw to the depth of the joint. As the members are curved, I used a wedge to line up the cut then just nibbled away the material as close to the line as possible. I used a wood rasp to clean up the bottoms of the trenches.

JOINING THE X-FRAMES

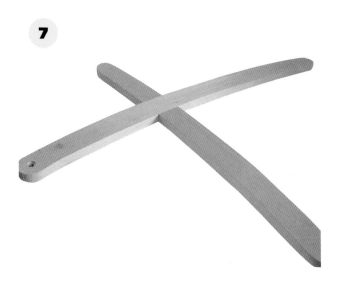

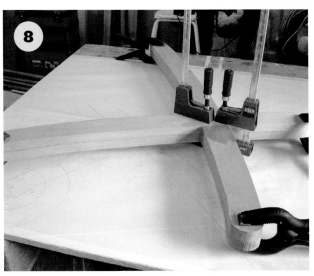

7 I next set up a drum sander in the drill press and set it to the depth of the joint and carefully sanded to the lines. This process was fiddly and took a long time but it's worth taking the time to produce a nice tight joint.

8 Once both joints were satisfactory, I applied some glue and clamped the two frames together. I used some spring clamps to help keep both frames aligned and set them aside to dry.

9 The handle of the trolley is a 1in (25mm) mahogany dowel so I turned to the lathe. After setting the blank in the lathe I rough turned it to round. Using a parting tool and an open end spanner, I turned a series of rings and then joined the rings to make the dowel.

10 To make it as uniform as possible, I wrapped a long block in sandpaper and sanded the dowel smooth. Finish sanding was done in the usual way and the blank set aside ready for trimming and fitting later. Back to the X-frames: after removing from the clamps I finished sanding both frames and rounded over all edges using a router fitted with a round-over bit.

MAKING THE WHEELS

11 The wheel rims start as four blocks mitred at each end. I cut the blanks at the tablesaw using my mitre gauge, but they could be cut by a power mitre saw or a radial arm saw.

12 Here are the finished wheel rim blanks.

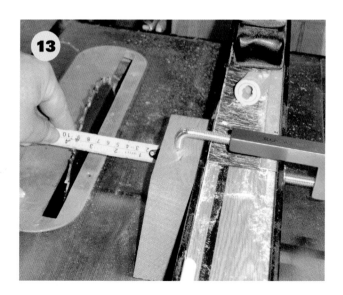

13 I cut the hub blanks, again on the tablesaw, using a stop block on the fence to avoid the work jamming on the blade. Here the guard has been removed for clarity, but you should never run a tablesaw with the guard removed.

14 I next clamped the blanks for one wheel together and pilot drilled for reinforcing screws, then screwed the blanks together. The process was repeated for the second wheel, and the hub blanks were then centred using small wedges.

15 Exact precision is not necessary; near enough is generally OK.

16 Placing a straight edge along the corners, the centre of the hub was marked. I used a pair of compasses to mark the outer rim of the wheel before using a '00' biscuit as a guide to mark the inner diameter. Next the hub diameter was marked. I marked the positions for the spokes. The depth of the spokes was marked on the hub and rim.

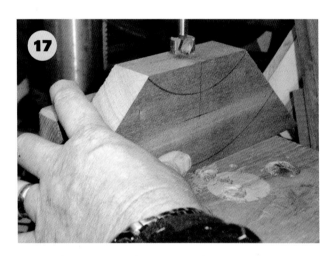

17 The wheel hubs were then removed, ready for drilling. It's a good idea to mark each set so as not to mix them up and keep the orientation the same. Once the blanks are separated, I transferred the spoke centrelines to the edges of the hub, ready for drilling. I also marked the centre of the blank with a marking gauge. The next step was to install a Forstner bit in the drill press and set the depth to the mark on the hub. After checking that the blank was square to the drill, the spoke holes were drilled. The rim blanks were drilled using the same techniques.

18 Next, I cut the inner diameter on the bandsaw. After all the blanks had been shaped, the sections were reassembled and the inner diameter refined on the oscillating drum sander. The hub was also cut to shape on the bandsaw and finished on the disc sander. The edges of the hubs and inner diameters were rounded over at the router table.

19 The spokes can be made from dowel stock but, since I have a lathe and plenty of scrap, I decided to turn my own dowels. I cut the spokes to length on the power mitre saw using a stop to ensure uniformity. With all the component parts prepared, it was time for assembly.

20 I first marked for biscuits, cut the slots and tried a dry fit to ensure everything fitted as it should. The dry fit was fine so with a coat of glue on all surfaces, some clamps and a few screws, the wheels were assembled and, after the excess glue had been cleaned, left to dry.

MAKING THE TRAYS

21 Once dry, the screws were removed and the outer diameter cut on the bandsaw. To ensure the wheels were concentric, I constructed a table on the disc sander with a slot set at 90° to the disc, both horizontally and vertically. I fixed a stop in this slot at the radius of the wheel, then fitted a pivot to the wheel centre point. The pivot was just a disc of hardwood with a small screw through the centre. I then slid the wheel across the table until it contacted the disc and then, by rotating the wheel, was able to sand the wheel to a true circle. After sanding off any marks, I rounded over the edges of both wheels. I next drilled the counter bore for the square part of the carriage bolt used for the axle and then the axle hole. All that remained was to insert the bolts into the wheels.

22 Now the relatively taxing bits are out of the way, it's time to take a look at the trays – when neatly put together, these will look stunning, so take care. In order to make the trays it was necessary to re-saw thick stock with the bandsaw using my widest blade and a centre-point fence. This was then jointed, thicknessed and ripped. I thicknessed a piece of stock to the width of the slats; the slats were then ripped at the bandsaw. After planing to thickness, I rounded over the edges at the router table.

23 To make the runners for the slide-out tray, after prepping the blank, I rebated each side at the router table then ripped the blank into two runners at the tablesaw – see page 46 on how to make the slide-out tray. I next mitred the tray frames at the mitre saw, using a stop block.

24 I built the trays using biscuits at the corners. The top tray cross-members were also fitted using biscuits. I nailed the corners to give a bit more support and, after checking for square, left the assembly to dry in the clamps. For the lower and lift-out trays, the corners are joined with mitres and biscuits like the upper tray but the slats fit into grooves machined into the sides of the trays. I machined these grooves at the router table.

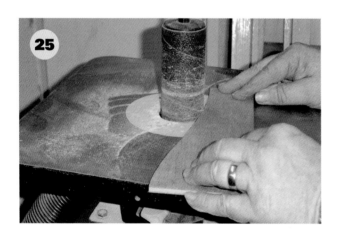

25 The lift out tray was a little more complicated. The ends needed to be shaped and I accomplished this by making a template from scrap ¼in (6mm) plywood. I used the template to mark out the ends and, after cutting at the bandsaw and smoothing at the drum sander, the tray pieces were ready for the hand holes. Using the top tray as a guide, I marked the position of the hand holes and, using the drill press, jigsaw, drum sander and router, finished the hand holes.

26 It is a good idea at this point to sand all the inner faces of the tray pieces. Gluing and nailing the first two corners was pretty straightforward but aligning and

fitting the 14 slats and 15 spacers and the fourth before the glue went off was somewhat challenging. Once pinned and clamped and checked for square, I left it to dry. The testing time came when the tray was removed from the clamps and test-fitted into the upper tray. Happily it fitted well. Before building the lower tray, I used the sides to mark the X-frames ready for final assembly. By sandwiching the sides between the X-frames and aligning everything on the template, I could mark what makes the inside face of each frame. I also took the opportunity to make the bottle holder for the lower tray so that I could drill the tray sides before assembly.

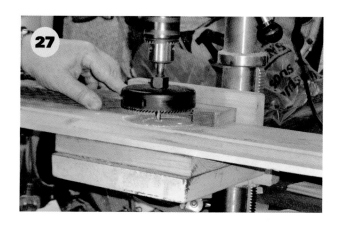

27 The bottle holder was made from iroko and, after the usual prep work, I shaped the two sections using a large hole-saw.

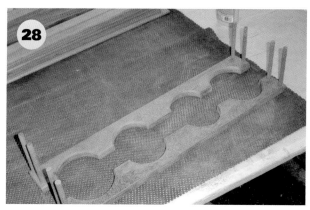

28 The bottle-holder supports were made from some more shop-made dowelling and to make life easier, I made a drilling jig, which allowed me to accurately position the holes in both the holder and the tray sides.

ASSEMBLY

29 With all the holes drilled, it was time to assemble the lower tray, using the same techniques as for the lift-out tray.

30 Now that all the main components were completed it was time to put it all together. First I sanded all the frames. I then placed one X-frame on the template and, using the marks made earlier, positioned the upper tray on the X-frame and drilled for screws using a combined drill and counter-bore bit. I then removed the tray, applied glue and secured the tray. I repeated the procedure for the lower tray then flipped the assembly cover and did the same with the second X-frame. At the drill press I made some plugs from some scrap pieces and fitted a plug to each screw hole, being sure to align the grain. I was pleased to see light at the end of the tunnel! The next job was to trim the plugs with a flush cutting saw and sand the plugs flush. A drop of glue in each of the pre-drilled holes and the bottle holder was fitted.

THE SLIDE-OUT TRAY

31 This tray is just a pair of stiles connected by a series of cross rails, all joined by biscuits and glue. Once I'd prepared the stock and cut all the pieces to size, I made a test fit. Once I was happy with the layout, I marked all the parts for biscuits. To make sure the tray dried as flat as possible, I clamped all the parts and the assembly to the bench.

32 When the glue had cured, I removed the assembly from the clamps and, using a router mat, sanded all the parts flush and smooth. I next routed a finger pull at each end of the tray, using a round-nosed bit in my router.

33 A few minutes at the disc sander gave the ends of the tray a nice profile and then it was just a case of fixing the runners under the upper tray.

34 The last job was to fit the wheels. I gave the entire project a liberal coat of teak oil and, after a few minutes, wiped off the excess. After a quick buff with a soft cloth, it was ready to go to work.

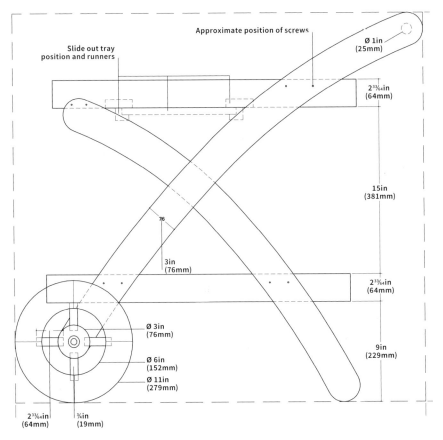

Approximate position of screws

Slide out tray position and runners

Ø 1in (25mm)

2³³⁄₆₄in (64mm)

15in (381mm)

76

3in (76mm)

2³³⁄₆₄in (64mm)

9in (229mm)

Ø 3in (76mm)

Ø 6in (152mm)

Ø 11in (279mm)

2³³⁄₆₄in (64mm)

¾in (19mm)

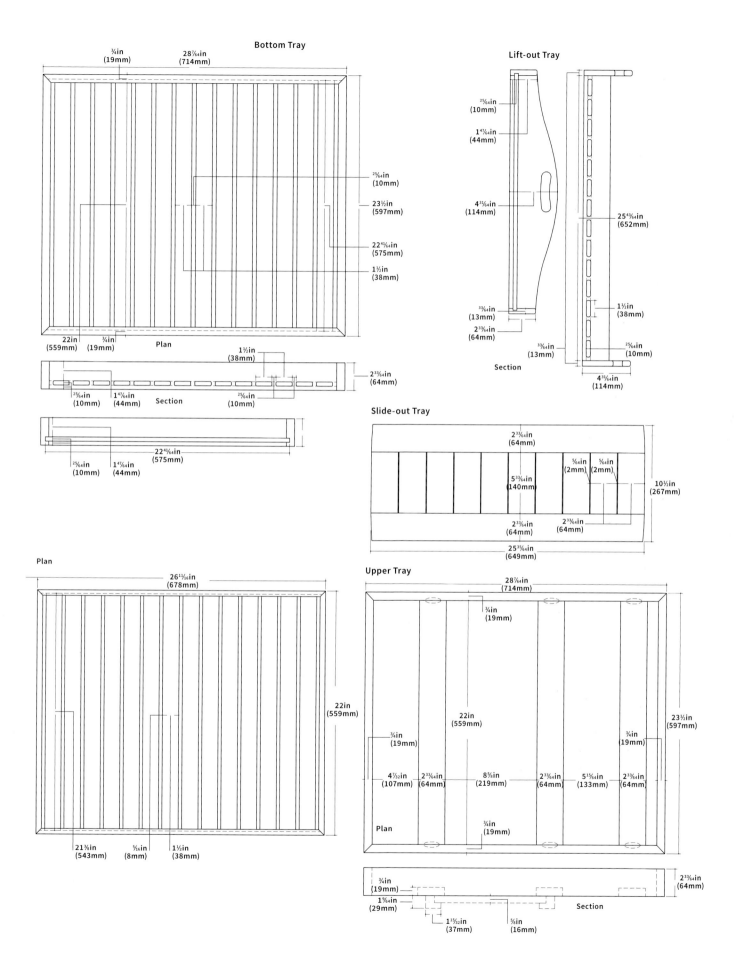

Bottom Tray

¾in
(19mm)

28⁷⁄₆₄in
(714mm)

²⁵⁄₆₄in
(10mm)

23½in
(597mm)

22⁴¹⁄₆₄in
(575mm)

1½in
(38mm)

22in
(559mm)

¾in
(19mm)

Plan

1½in
(38mm)

2²³⁄₆₄in
(64mm)

²⁵⁄₆₄in
(10mm)

1⁴⁷⁄₆₄in
(44mm)

Section

²⁵⁄₆₄in
(10mm)

²⁵⁄₆₄in
(10mm)

1⁴⁷⁄₆₄in
(44mm)

22⁴¹⁄₆₄in
(575mm)

Lift-out Tray

²⁵⁄₆₄in
(10mm)

1⁴⁷⁄₆₄in
(44mm)

4³¹⁄₆₄in
(114mm)

25⁴³⁄₆₄in
(652mm)

1½in
(38mm)

3³⁄₆₄in
(13mm)

2²³⁄₆₄in
(64mm)

3³⁄₆₄in
(13mm)

²⁵⁄₆₄in
(10mm)

Section

4³¹⁄₆₄in
(114mm)

Slide-out Tray

2²³⁄₆₄in
(64mm)

⁵⁄₆₄in
(2mm)

⁵⁄₆₄in
(2mm)

5³³⁄₆₄in
(140mm)

10½in
(267mm)

2²³⁄₆₄in
(64mm)

2²³⁄₆₄in
(64mm)

25³⁵⁄₆₄in
(649mm)

Plan

26¹¹⁄₁₆in
(678mm)

22in
(559mm)

21³⁄₈in
(543mm)

⁵⁄₁₆in
(8mm)

1½in
(38mm)

Upper Tray

28⁷⁄₆₄in
(714mm)

¾in
(19mm)

22in
(559mm)

23½in
(597mm)

¾in
(19mm)

¾in
(19mm)

4⁷⁄₃₂in
(107mm)

2²³⁄₆₄in
(64mm)

8⅝in
(219mm)

2²³⁄₆₄in
(64mm)

5¹⁵⁄₆₄in
(133mm)

2²³⁄₆₄in
(64mm)

Plan

¾in
(19mm)

2²³⁄₆₄in
(64mm)

¾in
(19mm)

1⁹⁄₆₄in
(29mm)

Section

1¹⁵⁄₃₂in
(37mm)

⅝in
(16mm)

WEATHERVANE

Keep an eye on wind direction with Fred and Julie Byrne's scrollsawn weathervane

What you need

- Scrollsaw fitted with a no. 5 blade
- Drill & drill bits
- ¼ & ¾in (6 & 18mm) marine plywood
- 48-72¹⁄₁₆in (1220-1830mm) length ¾in (18mm) dowel/broom handle (length depending on final positioning)
- Large nail
- Hammer
- 2 washers
- Waterproof glue
- Weatherproof paints/finishes

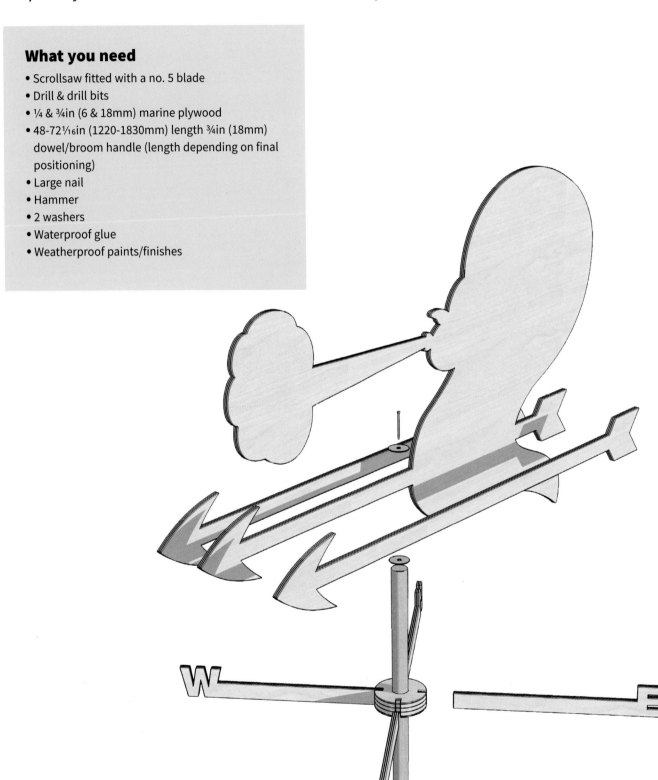

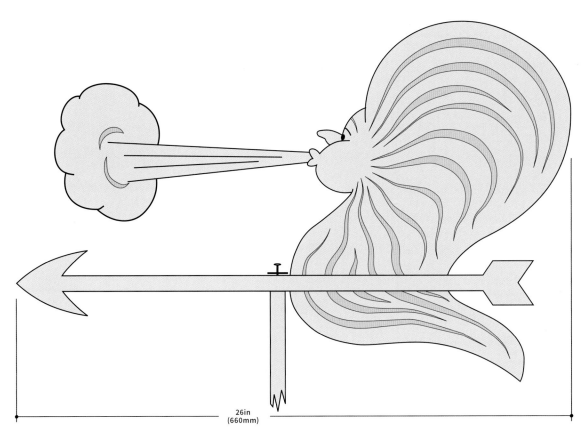

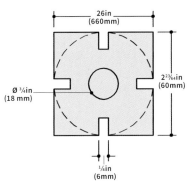

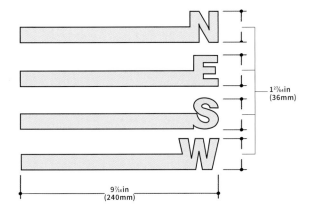

HOW TO MAKE IT

Enlarge the pattern until the main wind-blowing section measures approximately 26in (660mm). Attach this and the directional patterns to the ¼in (6mm) marine ply. Drill the blade entry holes for the interior cuts.

Cut out the entire pattern (including arrow) then cut two extra arrows (to be laminated to either side of the fixed arrow); because of the size you may need to make several cuts from different angles to complete the job.

Attach the pattern for the directional hub to the ¾in (18mm) ply, and either drill or cut out the ¾in (18mm) centre hole; cut the ¼in (6mm) slots before removing the corners. Glue and clamp the two additional arrows to either side of the main arrow, then glue the four directionals into the centre hub section. Allow to dry.

Measure 5²⁹⁄₃₂in (150mm) down from the top of the dowel and make a mark, apply a circle of glue, slide the hub down to the position and leave to dry. Drill a hole (slightly larger than the nail used) down through the centre part of the arrow and place a washer on either side.

Position the nail down through the washer and so on and hammer into the dowel, but not so tight that it stops the top from swinging freely. Paint the face on and apply a waterproof finish.

HERB PLANTER

Fred and Julie Byrne make this very useful herb holder

Designed to sit on the kitchen windowsill and be taken into the garden on nice sunny days especially for watering, this planter is a compact and convenient way to hold the fresh herbs you use most. Whether they are grown in your own garden or bought from the supermarket or garden centre, they'll be just at hand to use as you wish!

What you need

- Scrollsaw – no. 2 & 5 blades
- Pillar drill – ⅟₃₂in, ⅟₁₆in (0.8mm, 1.5mm) drill bits
- A quantity of ¼ & ⅛in (6 & 3mm) hardwood
- ⅞in (23mm) dowel (broom handle)
- PVA wood glue
- Glue stick/spray adhesive
- Masking tape
- Sandpaper & block
- Wood stain if needed
- Finish of choice

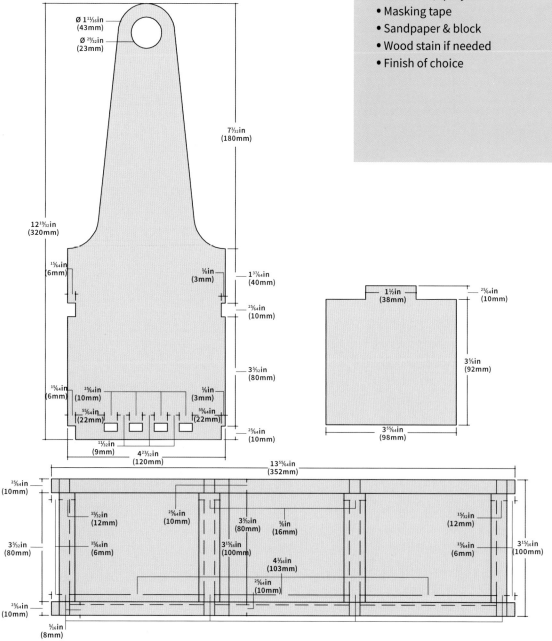

Cutting List

SIDE PANELS   2 @ ¼ x 4¾ x 12⅝in (6 x 120 x 320mm)
BACK PANEL   1 @ ¼ x 4 x 13⅞in (6 x 100 x 352mm)
FRONT PANEL   1 @ ⅛ x 4 x 13⅜in (3 x 100 x 340mm)
SLATS   1 @ ¼ x ⅜ x 13⅞in (6 x 10 x 352mm)

Front panel detail

INNER DIVIDING UPRIGHTS   4 @ ¼ x ⁵⁄₁₆ x 4in (6 x 8 x 100mm)
INNER LOWER SUPPORTS   3 @ ¼ x ⁵⁄₁₆ x 4¹⁄₃₂ (6 x 8 x 102.5mm)
UPPER & LOWER FASCIA   2 @ ⅛ x ⅜ x 13⅞in (3 x 10 x 352mm)
OUTER EDGE FASCIAS   2 @ ⅛ x ⅜ x 3⅛in (3 x 10 x 80mm)
CENTRE FASCIAS   2 @ ⅛ x ⅝ x 3⅛in (3 x 16 x 80mm)
HERB NAME PLATES   5 @ ⅛ x 3⅞ x 4¹⁄₆₄in (3 x 98 x 102mm)

1 Fit the scrollsaw with the no. 2 blade. Make a copy of each herb name you wish to use (see opposite page) and then using the glue stick, attach each name to a blank.

2 Using the pillar drill fitted with the ⅟₃₂in (0.8mm) drill bit, drill the blade entry holes into each letter.

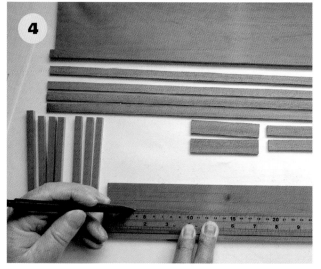

3 Cut around the inside line of the letter first and then the outside – that way the stress placed on the small connecting piece is kept to a minimum. Measure and draw out all the pieces from the cutting list

4 Continue to cut out all the ⅛in (3mm) pieces from the cutting list with the no. 2 blade, then change to the no. 5 blade before cutting out the ¼in (6mm) pieces.

Herbs Mint
Parsley Thyme
Basil Chives

SIDE PANELS

5 Using the masking tape, secure together the two ¼in (6mm) side panel pieces. Attach the pattern and the written word 'Herbs' detail if wished.

6 Apply the glue stick to the underside of the side panel pattern.

7 Again, drill the blades' entry holes using the ¹⁄₁₆in (1.5mm) drill bit and cut out the lettering as before.

8 Cut the lettering out first on the side panels. Next cut straight up both sides of the pattern.

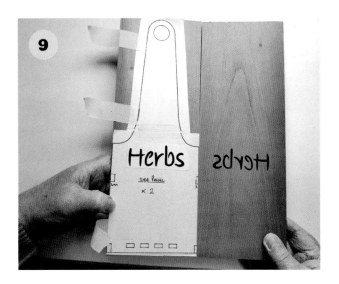

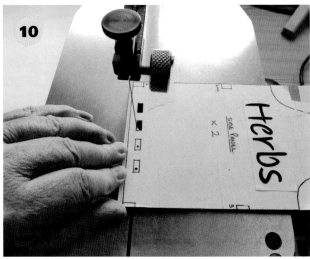

9 Separate these two side panels by peeling back the masking tape on the underside, then turn the underside piece completely over so that the word 'Herbs' is back to front – this will enable the word 'Herbs' to be facing in the correct position (to the outside) on the finished piece. This is necessary because the lower section of the side panels is slightly different, making them non-interchangeable.

10 Re-secure the two panels with masking tape and drill the remaining blade entry holes for the handle and four bottom slats.

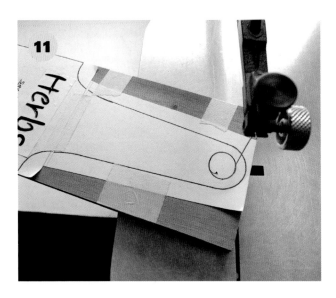

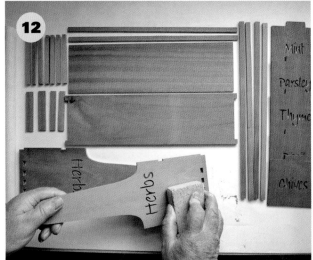

11 Cut out the pieces and finish the cutting by removing the four, ⅜in (10mm) notches on either side. Cut out the circle to take the handle.

12 Remove the patterns and then give all the pieces a light sanding going through the grits, then remove the fine dust with either a tack cloth or vacuum cleaner. Now is a good time for a dry run to make sure everything fits as it should, and to make any adjustments if needed. Next we applied a wood stain to the handle to match the red wood used, and then set it to one side to dry.

13 For gluing up, start by gluing the four inner upright dividers and three lower supports onto the front panel and allow to dry for a few minutes.

14 Next, glue on the six fascia pieces and wipe away any excess glue that may have oozed out, then set the front panel aside to dry.

15 Next, glue the four slats into the side panels and then the back panel.

16 Remember to wipe away the excess glue as you go, then slide and glue in the handle.

17 Lastly, glue the front panel into position and secure the whole thing with clamps, or in our case, use masking tape. Finally, give the whole piece a few coats of protective varnish, with a light de-nib between coats or, of course, a finish of your choice.

DOVECOTE

Anthony Bailey builds this lovely home for doves and pigeons

Here's a project to grace your back garden and hopefully entice those rare visitors, doves, or at the very least, some pigeons. Ever since the Roman Empire, wealthy people have encouraged doves to settle in dovecotes for their eggs, flesh and dung – not to mention the status value of the presence of these beautiful birds that are a symbol of peace and harmony. Some dovecotes were as big as small houses but to enhance your garden, this one is a more typical, down-to-earth example at a size you can afford without a mortgage!

The dovecote is built of exterior or marine ply with a bird-friendly finish designed to protect it from the elements. The whole exterior lifts off to give it a spring clean. This project uses 'template on template' as the technique for transferring each type of shape to the overall template, thus meaning you don't have to create lots of original shapes, so avoiding hard work and creeping inaccuracies.

What you need

- Sheet of ¼ or ⅜in (6 or 9mm) marine ply
- Additional ply or MDF for templates
- Roofing felt
- Large sheet of paper to draw plan
- Jigsaw or bandsaw
- Router with top bearing-guided cutter, bottom-guided template cutter, 'V' point, and bearing-guided bevel cutter

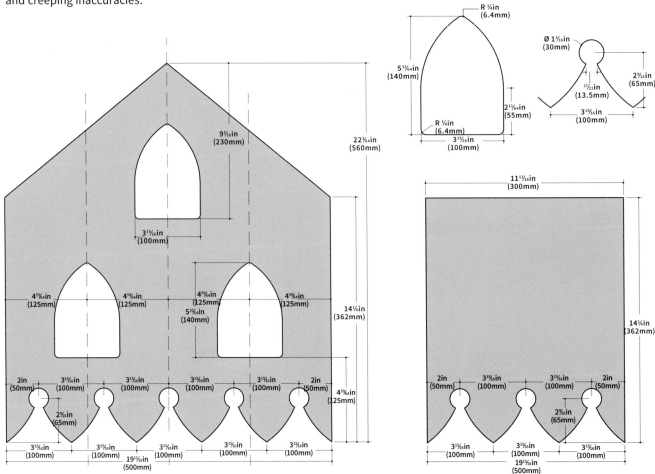

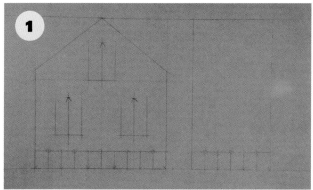

1 First make the template. Accurate laying out is essential – use the drawing opposite for all dimensions. I couldn't find any information about recommended sizes for dovecotes, but the ones shown are suitable. Draw out all positional information on a sheet of ¼ or ⅜in (6 or 9mm) MDF and then make a one-off freehand paper drawing of one of the arch shaped openings.

2 Carefully cut out the paper shape and draw around it on a smallish piece of ¼in (6mm) ply or MDF. If you run around the shape with your hand in the middle, the pencil cannot run under the paper, thus the inner edge of the drawn shape will be a smooth accurate curve. If you flip the paper over and use the same curve again, it must exactly mimic the first shape.

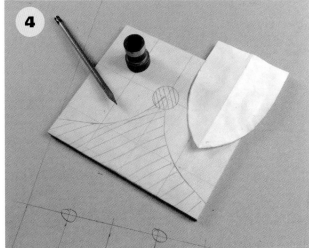

3 Use a jigsaw or bandsaw to cut close to the line, starting with an entrance and exit cut at the point. Cutting this way allows the blade to escape, but without any risk of the template flexing when the router runs around the shape. Smooth the arch shape with a wood file.

4 The spade shape along the bottom edge of the dovecote also starts with a single template. Draw 2in (50mm) spaced lines onto a board then, centred on the cross lines, mark a 1⅛in (30mm) diameter circle. Now fold the paper arch in half, lay it on the lines as shown and draw around it. Flip it over and draw the other side of the spade template – you will note that it creates a demi-spade shape at each side and not a whole spade. Allow a 'run-in' shape so that the cutter will follow the curves smoothly. Drill the circle out with a 1⅛in (28mm) spade bit and bandsaw the curves, then smooth back to the pencil lines with a wood file.

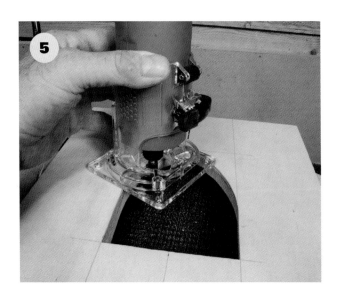

5 Place the arch template on the previously drawn positional lines on your large template. Pin it in place and use a top-bearing-guided cutter on your router, set down and pre-plunged so the bearing will run along your template. Move the router to the centre of the arch template ensuring the cutter is clear of the work, rest the base on one edge, switch on and tilt the router slowly to upright so the cutter plunges through the base. Ensure your work is held off the bench so you don't rout your bench! Now move the router to the edge of the template and run around clockwise. Do a complete circuit and the waste should drop away – switch off and lift out the waste piece. Repeat this operation for each arch.

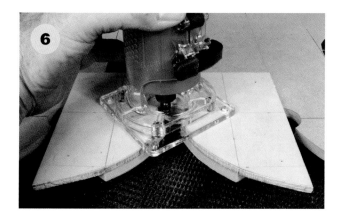

6 Now do the same thing with the spade template. Make sure you place it correctly so you end up with a demi-spade at each end and complete spade shapes in between. Note – the template must have enough space for a ½in (12mm) diameter top bearing-guided cutter to pass through the narrow neck into the circle at the top of the template. Start at one end and work along, machining each shape. This time, starting with a plunge cut is not required, of course. It is very gratifying to see each spade appear as it is accurately formed.

7 Repeat the spade operation on the intended end jig. By using two small templates we have created two larger full area templates. From these you can make not just one dovecote but as many as you wish, of course.

CONSTRUCTING THE DOVECOTE

8 This dovecote consists of two essential parts. The main carcass and roof are fixed together and must be able to lift off the back, which is a separate structure and fixed to the wall. Start by cutting the front and ends to width but leave overlength and square. Set up a V-groove cutter in the router table but remove the fence, as it won't allow for the correct distance for all the grooves – instead clamp a batten in place as a fence at 4in (100mm) in for the first groove. Do a test cut on a spare piece first and when you are satisfied the cut depth is correct, machine the first groove.

9 Turn the board around and do a repeat cut at the same distance. You can now do this with all the boards. The V-grooves on the carcass ends are complete but the front will need more grooves as it is wider. Reset the batten at 7⅞in (200mm) and repeat this exercise on the front board. You have now created a tongue-and-groove effect on all these boards apart from their edges. These take one half of the groove so keep the cutter height set but move the batten across so the cutter will create a recess in the batten half its diameter. Now machine the edges so they match the V-grooves. The front meeting corners are mitred together so these edges also need machining with the V-groove cutter.

10 Next, pin the template on the front board, mark the shapes, remove the template, and jigsaw the arches starting with a drilled hole – cut about ⅛in (3mm) in from the lines. Do the same with the spade shapes. Repeat this procedure with the ends, so all these components are ready to machine.

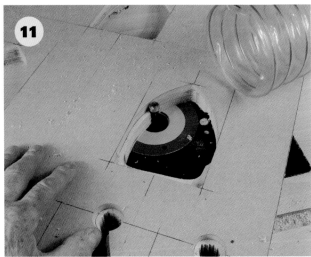

11 Set up a bottom-bearing-guided cutter in the router table with the fence removed – there should be no need for a lead-in pin. Refit each template ready to machine and make sure the bearing is the right height to run along the template. Start with the arches, ensuring you move into the cutter feed direction. You will need good extraction to draw up the chippings and dust.

12 Now repeat the operation, this time machining the spade shapes. Work carefully around the shape, particularly the small circular cutouts. Run around a second time to ensure the shape exactly follows the template.

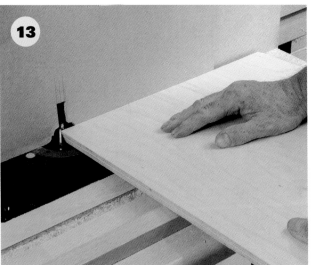

13 Machine the bevel on the meeting ends of the two roof sections. This is done on the router table using a bevel cutter and batten on the table to get the required angle. Do not let the cutter remove the entire edge as it will cause the edge to be tapered or uneven as it gets machined.

14 Now pin the sides to the front of the dovecote and the roof to the sides using exterior glue along the long meeting edges. Make sure they are perpendicular to the front. Pin and glue battens inside the corners to increase their strength. Leave to set after removing any surplus glue.

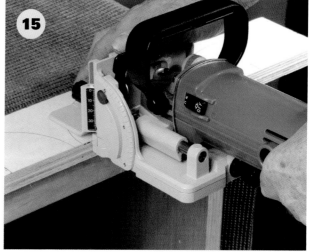

15 Each ledge for the dove openings is a semicircle and is bandsawn out to shape then sanded. After that, a small radius is run around the curved edges. Once machined, these are biscuit jointed to the front of the dovecote flush with the bottom of each arch. Note – it makes sense to cut the biscuit slots in a long piece of ply, cutting out the individual shapes afterwards.

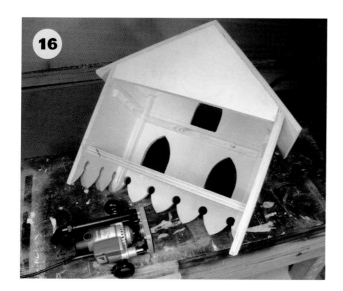

16 The bottom floor position is marked around the inside of the dovecote. It has to fit around the front corner reinforcement battens and allow for the removable back panel which is required for cleaning the dovecote out periodically. The top floor sits on small battens – the edges of which I planed up with a benchtop planer – and the floor can be pulled out using a fingerpull in the floor.

17 Once the dovecote is fully assembled it is ready for sanding and applying a full-gloss paint system. Then it can be attached to a garden wall or fence, ready for the new residents.

SMALL GARDEN TABLE

Jim Robinson builds a great little table for the summer

I wanted a small folding table to use in the garden and had recently been given some old teak laboratory benches. After cutting them into reasonable lengths, I was left with some smaller lengths, which I thought would be ideal for a small project like this.

Incidentally, this table is versatile in that it can be used as an occasional stool. Alternative woods to use would be oak and ash. The construction remains the same if you vary the overall size – the only advice I can give is that if you vary the size, make some trial legs out of MDF so that you can experiment and get the folding action correct with the different leg length.

The problem with using reclaimed material is the surface dirt and finish make the detection of small pins and so on, difficult. However, the cost of more frequent sharpening of planer blades is more than offset by the amount saved on buying the wood, and then there is the satisfaction gained by recycling.

Cutting list

Allowances made on lengths only

TOP SIDES	2 @ 11 x 2 x ⅞in (279 x 50 x 22mm)	END APRON	2 @ 13 x 1½ x ⅞in (331 x 38 x 22mm)
TOP ENDS	2 @ 15 x 2 x ⅞in (381 x 50 x 22mm)	LEGS	4 @ 19 x 1½ x ¾in (483 x 38 x 19mm)
TOP SLATS	6 @ 11½ x 1¼ x ½in (292 x 32 x 12mm)	STRETCHERS	3 @ 10 x ⅞ x ¾in (254 x 22 x 19mm)
SIDE APRON	2 @ 14½ x 1½ x ⅞in (368 x 38 x 22mm)		

Also required: 4 coach bolts, ⅛in (3mm) diameter washers & nuts – length depends on finished thickness of wood used

1 The teak was well over 1in (25mm) in thickness, so there was little difficulty in achieving the desired sizes. The top consists of an outer surround or apron with thinner slats fixed between the two ends.

2 I planed and thicknessed the 2in (50mm) wide wood for the surround – and made them slightly longer at this stage to trim them later.

3 The slats are ½in (12mm) thick and I was able to resaw them to obtain two widths from the original thickness. If the wood you are using is nominal 1in (25mm) sawn material, you may have to settle for somewhat thinner slats.

4 When resawing, make sure the sides are planed square, and use a sharp ½in (12mm) or wider bandsaw blade with no more than 4 or 5 skip saw teeth to the inch (4 or 5 per 25mm).

5 Hold the wood well against the fence and proceed slowly, giving the sawdust plenty of time to clear. The old wood I used stayed flat but if your wood is new it might bow slightly, which can mean you have to plane a little more of the thickness away.

Above you can see Jim's elegant folding points.

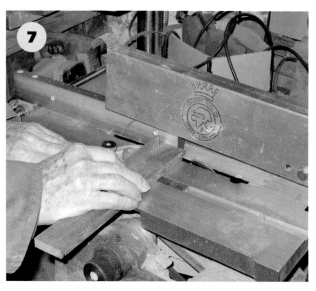

6 With a router fitted with a ¼in (6mm) straight bit, take out a groove ⁵⁄₁₆in (8mm) deep, starting ⅜in (10mm) from the top of the end surround pieces, or slightly less if the thickness of your slats are less. The object is to finish with the top of your slats flush with the surround. Cut the side pieces forming the surround and the slats to the length between the end pieces of the top, plus ⅝in (16mm) to allow for the tongue or tenon at each end.

7 To form the tenon at the ends of the slats, cut the shoulder – I used a table saw with the depth and fence set.

8 Then use a bandsaw with the fence set to complete the tenon.

9 The top can now be assembled. Apply a waterproof glue to the grooves before inserting the side frames and slats so that the spaces between are even. The tenon may seem small, but this joint is strengthened when the side and end rails are fixed to the underside of the tabletop. Keep the top in the clamps until set, then make the side and end apron pieces and screw these in position. Do not use glue at this stage because it is easier to remove the side apron so that the bolt hole for the legs to swivel on can be drilled using the bench drill.

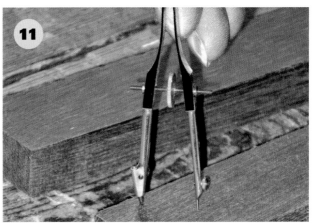

10 Once the glue has gone off and after the end pieces are cut to length, give the top a good sanding.

11 Make the legs 1½in (38mm) wide and round the leg tops – the ends nearest the tabletop. I used a small pair of spring-bow compasses to draw the outline before cutting and sanding to shape.

12 In two of the legs, drill a clearance hole for the coach bolts, centred at the same place as the compass point in step 11. The holes in the legs are centred ¾in (19mm) from the end and side. In order that the legs are free to pivot easily, drill a hole in the side apron ⅞in (22mm) from the underside of the tabletop and the internal corner where the end and side aprons meet.

13 I made a template for the legs out of MDF to ensure that the legs folded and were correctly positioned. If you are making the table a different size, then this step will be essential. When you are satisfied with the MDF legs, the teak legs can be drilled with the central clearance

hole, so that each pair of legs can swivel around a coach bolt. The inner set of legs have three stretchers to prevent racking but before making these, it is best to fit the teak legs in place so that the measurement for the stretchers can be checked. To assemble the legs, place the coach bolt in the hole drilled in the side apron, then after first placing a spacer washer on the bolt, place the legs in position. Next, use a bolt passed through the holes drilled near the leg centres to join the adjacent legs in place, after first using three spacing washers to separate the legs where they cross so that they can move freely and will not engage the coach bolt nuts when being folded.

14 Now measure the distance between the legs so the stretchers can be made. Before taking the legs apart, place a ruler at the distance required from the ground and parallel to the seat top, so that the length of the legs and the angle at the base can be indicated, ready for cutting and sawing.

The full extent of Jim's elegant fold-down table legs.

15 I turned ½in (12mm) pins on each end of the stretchers, so that they could be glued into holes drilled in the legs. Use the long corner of a skew chisel to make a shoulder.

16 Then turn the pin using a parting tool. If you do not have a lathe, you will have to chop a small mortise to take a tenon made on the stretcher ends.

17 After gluing the stretchers in place, glue and clamp the legs.

The legs of Jim's table in the folded-away position.

18-19 In order to stop the nuts coming loose, cut the bolts off flush with the nut, and then give the nut another complete turn. Next, use a small hammer, ball or cross pein if you have one, to rivet the

projecting bolt over, so that the nut cannot be removed. I used a small hook and eye to prevent the legs coming away from the top, if it is lifted by the top without holding the legs.

FINISHING

20 Teak, even when reclaimed, can be somewhat oily, so I let the table weather a while before applying a coat of tung oil diluted 50/50 with white spirit to aid penetration. I find this better than proprietary teak oil.

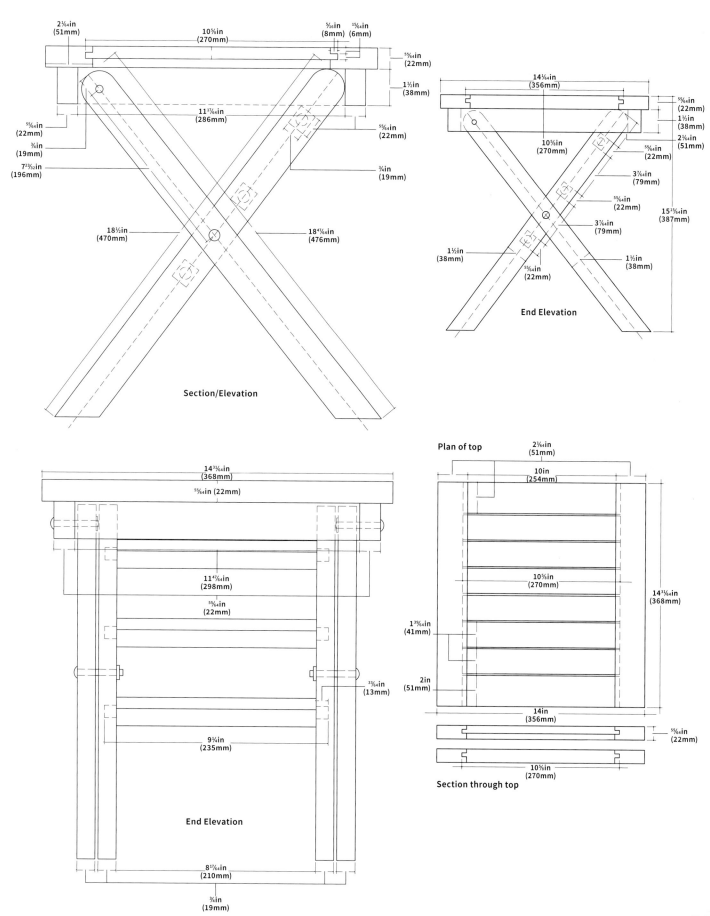

2¼₆₄in
(51mm)

10⅝in
(270mm)

⁵⁄₁₆in
(8mm)

¹⁵⁄₆₄in
(6mm)

⁵⁵⁄₆₄in
(22mm)

1½in
(38mm)

11¹⁷⁄₆₄in
(286mm)

⁵⁵⁄₆₄in
(22mm)

⁵⁵⁄₆₄in
(22mm)

¾in
(19mm)

7²³⁄₃₂in
(196mm)

¾in
(19mm)

18½in
(470mm)

18⁴⁷⁄₆₄in
(476mm)

Section/Elevation

14¹⁄₆₄in
(356mm)

⁵⁵⁄₆₄in
(22mm)

1½in
(38mm)

2¼₆₄in
(51mm)

10⅝in
(270mm)

⁵⁵⁄₆₄in
(22mm)

3⁷⁄₆₄in
(79mm)

⁵⁵⁄₆₄in
(22mm)

15¹⁵⁄₆₄in
(387mm)

3⁷⁄₆₄in
(79mm)

1½in
(38mm)

⁵⁵⁄₆₄in
(22mm)

1½in
(38mm)

End Elevation

14³¹⁄₆₄in
(368mm)

⁵⁵⁄₆₄in (22mm)

11⁴⁷⁄₆₄in
(298mm)

⁵⁵⁄₆₄in
(22mm)

³³⁄₆₄in
(13mm)

9¼in
(235mm)

End Elevation

8¹⁷⁄₆₄in
(210mm)

¾in
(19mm)

Plan of top

2¼₆₄in
(51mm)

10in
(254mm)

10⅝in
(270mm)

14³¹⁄₆₄in
(368mm)

1³⁹⁄₆₄in
(41mm)

2in
(51mm)

14in
(356mm)

⁵⁵⁄₆₄in
(22mm)

10⅝in
(270mm)

Section through top

PICNIC BENCH

Alan Holtham designs and builds his unusual version of a garden favourite

This is a great outdoor project that will only take a couple of days to build, and will bring hours of pleasure to your summer alfresco dining experiences! Despite its simple appearance, quite a lot of thought went into the design process, as I had a number of criteria to fulfil, while trying not to make the job too complicated.

For a start, I wanted to avoid the standard A-frame style that is commonly used in every pub beer garden and picnic area the world over. Although a well tried and tested design, my issue with it is that you have to 'thread' yourself through it onto a seat – not ideal for your older guests. Secondly, I wanted a table that has wheelchair access for a friend of mine, rather than have him stuck sideways on the end of a conventional picnic table. Thirdly, the table had to be quick and easy to dismantle so it could be put away during the winter and, fourthly, it had to be made within a small budget, using standard off-the-shelf material and minimal power tools.

Cutting list

FRAME	3 @ $82\frac{43}{64}$ x $3\frac{3}{4}$ x $1\frac{13}{16}$in (2100 x 95 x 46mm)
LEGS	6 @ $35\frac{7}{16}$ x $3\frac{3}{4}$ x $1\frac{3}{4}$in (Ex 900 x 95 x 46mm)
TOP SUPPORTS	3 @ $17\frac{29}{32}$ x $3\frac{3}{4}$ x $1\frac{3}{4}$in (455 x 95 x 46mm)
TOP SUPPORT FRAME	6 @ $19\frac{31}{64}$ x $1\frac{13}{16}$ x $1\frac{13}{16}$in (Ex 495 x 46 x 46mm)
TOP SLATS	7 @ $37\frac{13}{32}$ x $3\frac{3}{4}$ x $1\frac{37}{64}$in (950 x 95 x 40mm)
TOP SLATS	2 @ $26\frac{31}{32}$ x $3\frac{3}{4}$ x $1\frac{37}{64}$in (Ex 685 x 95 x 40mm)
TOP SLATS	2 @ $13\frac{25}{64}$ x $3\frac{3}{4}$ x $1\frac{37}{64}$in (Ex 340 x 95 x 40mm)
SEAT	9 @ $39\frac{3}{8}$in x $3\frac{3}{4}$ x $1\frac{37}{64}$in (1000 x 95 x 40mm)
SEAT BACK	3 @ $39\frac{3}{8}$in x $3\frac{3}{4}$ x $1\frac{37}{64}$in (1000 x 95 x 40mm)

1 With all this in mind, and after some extensive internet research, I settled on a hexagonal design with three double seats that are easily accessible from either side. For the material, I used 3¾ x 1¾in (95 x 46mm) carcassing wood which is relatively cheap, and although not finished to the standard of PAR material, is certainly a lot smoother than rough sawn. It also has the corners machined to a smooth radius, which makes the finished project a lot more user-friendly, with a minimum of work.

2 The slight disadvantage is that each piece has regular ink markings along its length, carrying information about the grade. As I was going to paint the finished bench, this was not really an issue, but if you anticipate using a clear finish then either sand off the printing, or feed each piece through a thicknesser, taking off just a very light pass. There is also a tanalized option for extra durability, but this is considerably more expensive.

3 As the basic shape of the table is hexagonal, you need to make a lot of angled cuts, so a mitre saw is almost essential but before you start, make a trial cut to check that the angle is spot on and the cut is square.

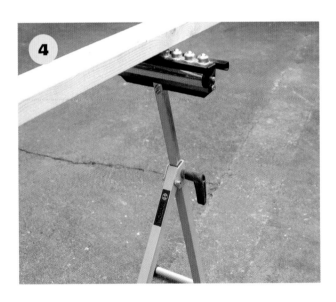

4 To minimize waste, I bought 165¾in (4.2m) lengths of material which are quite awkward to handle on your own, but a roller stand or trestle will make the sawing process easier and also safer. Roller stands are like a third hand in the workshop and to my mind, are worth their weight in gold, particularly the ball type.

Making the joint jig

You need to calculate the distance between the two MDF guide strips, and for this you need to work out the guidebush margin (gbm) which depends on the relative diameters of the cutter and guidebush you're using.
Guide bush margin = (Guide bush diameter – cutter diameter) ÷ 2

A All you need is a couple of pieces of wood about 13¾in (350mm) long to straddle either side of the workpiece, and a couple of pieces of MDF with edges machined perfectly straight.

B Using a scrap of the actual workpiece material as a spacer, screw the first piece of MDF across the two jig components at the required 60° angle.

C For an internal template such as this, the margin must be added to each edge of the workpiece dimension, and you can then attach the second strip accordingly. If you're making an external template where the guidebush follows the outside edge, subtract the margin from each edge of the workpiece dimension.

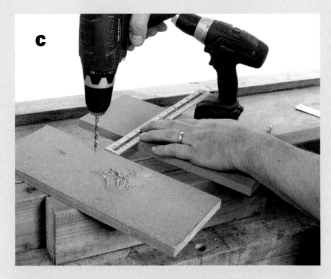

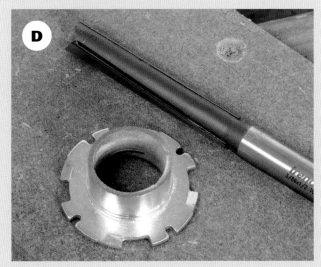

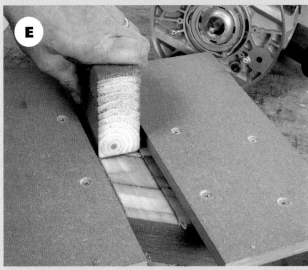

D In this case, I was using a 1⅛in (30mm) guidebush and a ½in (13mm) cutter.
So the gbm is: 1⅛ – ½in (30 – 13mm) ÷ 2 = ⁵⁄₁₆in (8.5mm)

E With the jig assembled, make a few trial cuts to check how well the joint fits. Don't try and be too clever in making this really tight, or you will have difficulty assembling the joint, particularly if the wood gets damp and swells.

F It needs to be a sliding fit that just requires a light tap to get it seated, and it took me three attempts to get this perfect, as you can see in this photograph.

G The trick is to initially make the gap between the jig guide rails slightly too narrow, as you can then easily unscrew one and plane a fraction off to ease the joint. It is much harder to close up the gap if you have initially made it too big.

5 Lay out the three components of the main frame and mark the positions of the half-lap joints – and remember the joints need to be cut on opposite edges on each piece. As the whole structure of the bench depends on these joints being good, I decided on a method using the router to form the perfect joint. This produces a perfectly sized cutout with minimal effort, but it will require you to make a very simple template jig (previous page) to use with a long straight cutter and a guidebush in the router.

6 It would be very messy and time-consuming to rout out the whole joint so with the trenching stop on your mitre saw set up for depth, cut to within a fraction of the marked joint.

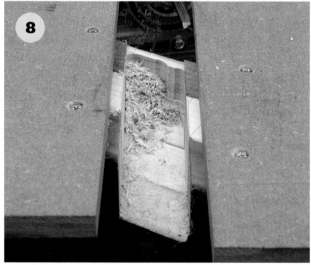

7 Use a chisel to knock out the majority of the waste, taking care not to split the waste off too deep.

8 Then clamp the router jig in place and machine out the joint to the perfect width and depth.

9 The triangle frame should now fit together, requiring just a light tap with a rubber mallet to seat the joints properly.

10 For the sake of neatness, I used a small roundover bit in the router to radius the cut edges of the joint to match the existing edge profile.

11 The six legs can now be cut to length with the 15° angle on one end to produce the necessary inclination.

12 I could have cut this same angle on the top end of each leg as well, but thought a double angle would look neater.

13 All cut ends and edges are radiused to match the long edges and for jobs like this, I love using my palm router, which is so light and manoeuvrable.

14 Although I did not require a super-smooth finish, as it is a picnic bench meant for outdoors, a quick brush over using a random-orbit sander with a 120-grit disc made a huge difference to both the feel and appearance of the wood, which was worth doing.

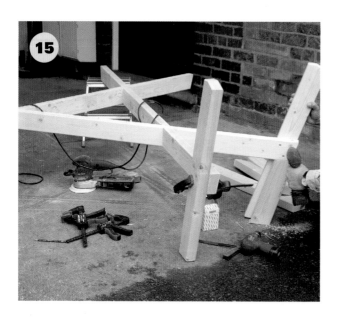

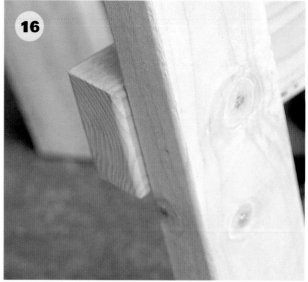

15 Now you can start the assembly, which is initially quite tricky if you are working on your own, but I used a combination of paint tins and blocks to hold the main frame level while screwing on the legs. Use a spacer to ensure that each cross rail is fixed at the right height on each leg.

16 I think it always looks neater in this situation if you deliberately overlap the pieces to be joined, rather than try and get them flush, but this is a matter of personal opinion – decide for yourself which you think looks best.

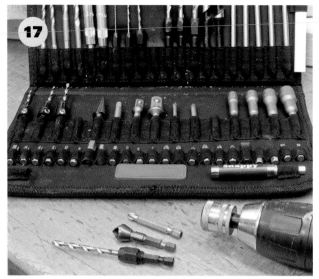

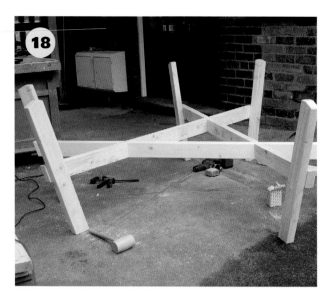

17 Another good tip, particularly if you only have one drill and are drilling, countersinking and screwdriving in quick succession, is to use a quick change chuck system. This allows you to make very quick changes to the drill set-up and will recoup its costs in no time.

18 The basic frame soon took shape, a process made so much easier if you have a perfectly flat surface to work on. If not, use wedges under each leg to avoid introducing distortions.

19 The table's upright supports require careful shaping to be a close fit in each apex. I could not think of a way of doing this using a machine or power tool, so I resorted to cutting them by hand.

20 The uprights are then just screwed in place – I used two screws from one side of the joint and one from the other.

21 The tabletop frame is made from the same material but ripped down the middle – a single screw is enough to hold each corner joint as it all stiffens up when you fix on the top boards.

22 So that's the framework complete and now it just requires covering to form the seats and tabletop. To make the whole thing appear lighter, I reduced the rest of the material down to 1⅝in (40mm), which is still plenty strong enough but stopped it all looking too chunky.

23 The slats for the table are screwed through from the underside using hardboard spacers to maintain an even gap. Where possible, screw through into one slat from either side of a frame joint to increase its rigidity.

24 The challenge is to ensure that the smallest part of the hexagon top is still big enough to get a secure fixing onto the frame.

25 With the top complete, radius all the edges as before, and then give it a thorough sanding, as the wood is not the best quality and does feature some quite large knots and areas of torn grain.

26 The seat is made from three slats fixed from the top, with angled ends to make it easier to walk in and sit down.

27 The back is just a single slat screwed onto the angle of the legs. I did consider letting this in to produce a bigger bearing surface but in reality, just a single screw through the arris of each leg seemed to be quite sufficient.

28 If you anticipate using a parasol, drill a suitably sized hole in the middle of the table and then use your router to radius the top edge for a neater appearance.

29 The completed bench. It took me about 12 hours to get to this stage, and what had been a rough sketch with approximate dimensions actually worked out quite well! I was particularly pleased that the seat arrangement still allowed easy wheelchair access as required in the original brief.

30 Now it was just a question of dismantling and reassembling on site. It only took about 10 minutes with my drill driver to reduce the bench to its component parts.

31 To finish, I used a coloured preservative which I've always found to withstand the weather well, even in direct sunlight. Apply this is as you reassemble the bench, so that all the joint surfaces can be covered as well.

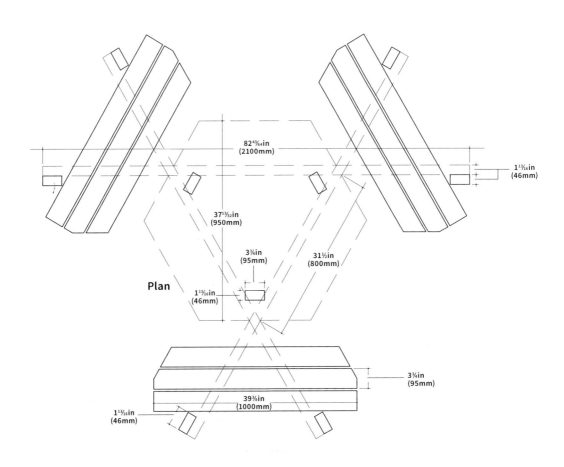

82⁴⁵⁄₆₄in
(2100mm)

1¹³⁄₁₆in
(46mm)

37¹³⁄₃₂in
(950mm)

3¾in
(95mm)

31½in
(800mm)

Plan

1¹³⁄₁₆in
(46mm)

3¾in
(95mm)

39³⁄₈in
(1000mm)

1¹³⁄₁₆in
(46mm)

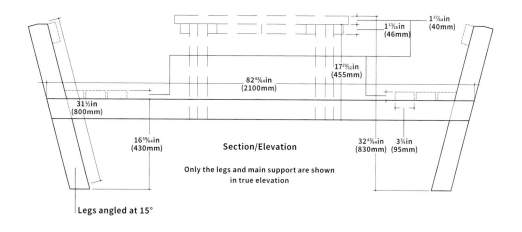

1³⁷⁄₆₄in
(40mm)

1¹³⁄₁₆in
(46mm)

17²⁹⁄₃₂in
(455mm)

82⁴⁵⁄₆₄in
(2100mm)

31½in
(800mm)

16⁵⁹⁄₆₄in
(430mm)

Section/Elevation

Only the legs and main support are shown
in true elevation

32⁴³⁄₆₄in
(830mm)

3¾in
(95mm)

Legs angled at 15°

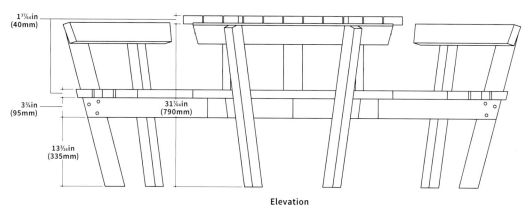

1³⁷⁄₆₄in
(40mm)

3¾in
(95mm)

13³⁄₁₆in
(335mm)

31⁷⁄₆₄in
(790mm)

Elevation

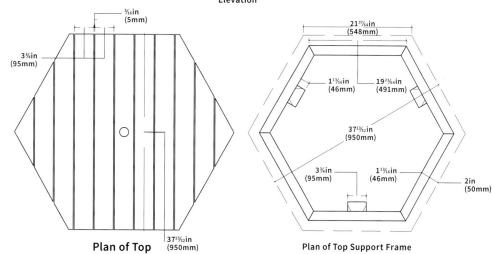

³⁄₁₆in
(5mm)

3¾in
(95mm)

Plan of Top

37¹³⁄₃₂in
(950mm)

21³⁷⁄₆₄in
(548mm)

1¹³⁄₁₆in
(46mm)

19²¹⁄₆₄in
(491mm)

37¹³⁄₃₂in
(950mm)

3¾in
(95mm)

1¹³⁄₁₆in
(46mm)

2in
(50mm)

Plan of Top Support Frame

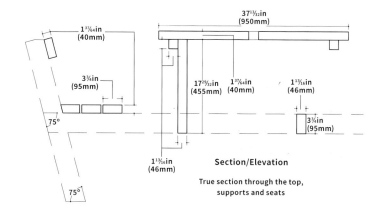

37¹³⁄₃₂in
(950mm)

1³⁷⁄₆₄in
(40mm)

3¾in
(95mm)

75°

17²⁹⁄₃₂in
(455mm)

1³⁷⁄₆₄in
(40mm)

1¹³⁄₁₆in
(46mm)

3¾in
(95mm)

1¹³⁄₁₆in
(46mm)

75°

Section/Elevation

True section through the top,
supports and seats

BAT BOX

Andy Standing creates a belfry-inspired bat box

Making boxes for birds or bats can be a pretty simple process. You can just nail together several crudely sawn boards and the birds or bats will be happy. But perhaps you want to take a little more trouble and make something more decorative and with a theme. While designing this bat box, I tried to imagine a theme the bats could identify with. Dracula perhaps? Halloween? No. Where do you find bats? In the belfry, of course. So here is my bat box design with a bit of a belfry feel to it.

You will need

- 1 x plank
- Dremel Versatip
- Tenon saw
- Blowlamp
- Tablesaw
- Mitre guide
- Pillar drill
- Drum sander
- Jigsaw
- Coping saw
- Cutter
- Router
- Side fence
- Pocket hole jig

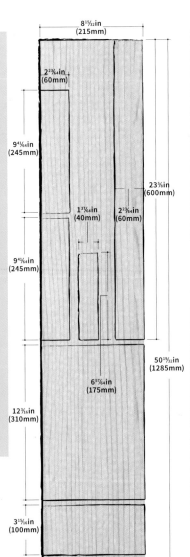

8$^{15}\!/_{32}$in
(215mm)

2$^{23}\!/_{64}$in
(60mm)

9$^{41}\!/_{64}$in
(245mm)

23$^{5}\!/_{8}$in
(600mm)

1$^{37}\!/_{64}$in
(40mm)

2$^{23}\!/_{64}$in
(60mm)

9$^{41}\!/_{64}$in
(245mm)

6$^{57}\!/_{64}$in
(175mm)

50$^{19}\!/_{32}$in
(1285mm)

12$^{3}\!/_{16}$in
(310mm)

3$^{15}\!/_{16}$in
(100mm)

9$^{41}\!/_{64}$in
(245mm)

1 Begin by marking out your plank.

2 Crosscut the components to length.

3 Rip them to width.

4 The backboard needs to have grooves cut into it so that the bats will have something to grip on to. Mark out a series of lines with a try square, about ¾in (20mm) apart.

5 The grooves can be cut with a router and side fence. Use a ³⁄₁₆in (4mm) diameter straight cutter and set the depth to ³⁄₁₆in (4mm) as well.

6 When routing the grooves, be sure to hold the side fence tight against the edge of the board to keep the grooves straight. The board is supported here on a vacuum clamp.

7 The finished backboard.

8 Now fix the side panels to the front board. Use a pocket hole jig to drill the sides.

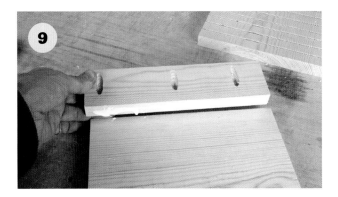

9 Use exterior grade waterproof glue to fix the sides.

10 Then screw into place.

11 Screw the bottom board in place. It must be ¾in (20mm) narrower than the sides to allow a small space for the bats to squeeze through.

12 Glue and screw the backboard in position.

13 The crenellations around the top of the belfry are made on separate boards that are then fixed to the edge of the top panel. The cutouts between the uprights are ²³⁄₃₂in (18mm) wide and ¾in (20mm) deep and the uprights are ¾in (20mm) wide. The semicircles below

are marked out using a small coin. Marking this out can be quite a fiddly process. Make sure you do it accurately otherwise the corner joints won't work properly.

14 Use a jigsaw or coping saw to remove the waste.

15 A small drum sander mounted in a pillar drill can be used to clean up the semicircles.

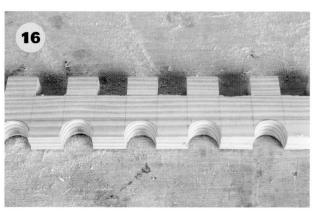

16 It should end up looking like this.

17 Carefully work out the position of the corner joints and cut the mitres using a tenon saw and a mitre box, or a tablesaw with a mitre guide.

18 Arrange the parts around the top panel and mark the length.

19 Cut to length.

20 Glue and pin the pieces around the top panel. Set the base of the cutouts flush with the top of the panel.

21 With the top completed, I decided to decorate the box with a bell tower window and a door at the base.

22 I used a Dremel Versatip gas torch to burn the images onto the box. Draw out the design in pencil first.

23 Filling in the windows with a pattern. We are approaching the limits of my artistic expertise here!

24 To give the box a more aged and interesting look, I singed parts of it with the blowlamp.

The finished belfry. Now where are those bats?

MINI WHEELBARROW

James Hatter creates a toy to capture a young gardener's imagination, which can also be used as a display feature

I made a toy wheelbarrow for my young grandson as he was keen to have a wheelbarrow like his dad's. The design of the wheelbarrow has a Victorian feel about it, and was painted for protection and colour. Although this is designed and constructed as a toy, taking into account the Toy Safety Standards, an alternative use would be as a display wheelbarrow. Filled with flowering plants it would make a fine decoration on any patio.

SAFETY FIRST

Toy version

The toy wheelbarrow has been constructed and finished to ensure that it does not pose a risk to the young user. Clear guidance is found in the European Toy Standards EN71, and these have been adhered to. If yours is for use and not display, please adhere to your local standards too. Essentially, the structure must not use hazardous materials, or have features that can cause injury. These standards have been followed in the construction of the wheelbarrow featured in this project. The materials used include plywood and softwood, all edges have been rounded, and finished with low-VOC water-based paints. The screws, and other fixing items have had PVA adhesive added to give protection against becoming loose, and wood plugs or filler are used to cover most screw heads. Having taken all steps to ensure safety, it is still advisable that there is a responsible person present when this toy is being used.

The plywood used in this project is ½in (12mm) Far Eastern WBP type; this is suitable for both versions as it uses water-resistant adhesives to bind the ply together. This type of plywood is usually durable and economically priced; it does, however, often have voids visible from the edges, and these will require filling if found.

Display version

For this application, preservatives and external finishes can be used, giving added protection for continuous outdoor use. You will also need to use exterior-grade adhesives and it would be worth cutting drainage holes in the base of the wheelbarrow. If the display is to remain static then a simple fixed wooden wheel could be used instead of the rotating arrangement described for the toy version. A display version could be made larger by applying a multiplier to the dimensions given; the angles will remain the same. Potted plants could be placed in the wheelbarrow, and the pots hidden by bark chippings. If compost is to be loaded directly into the barrow, then it would be advisable to line the barrow with a plastic layer.

Cutting list

HANDLES	2 @ 33$\frac{55}{64}$ x 1$\frac{47}{64}$ x ¾in (860 x 44 x 19mm)
SPINDLE SUPPORTS	2 @ 4$\frac{3}{32}$ x 1$\frac{47}{64}$ x 1$\frac{19}{64}$in (104 x 44 x 33mm)
CROSS PIECEs	1 @ 9$\frac{7}{16}$ x 1$\frac{47}{64}$ x ¾in (240 x 44 x 19mm)
	1 @ 6$\frac{7}{64}$ x 1$\frac{47}{64}$ x ¾in (155 x 44 x 19mm)
LEGS	2 @ 13$\frac{3}{16}$ x 2$\frac{19}{32}$ x 1$\frac{19}{64}$in (335 x 66 x 33mm)
SUPPORTS	2 @ 5$\frac{5}{16}$ x 2$\frac{19}{32}$ x 1$\frac{19}{64}$in (135 x 66 x 33mm)
PANEL BOTTOM	1 @ 13$\frac{47}{64}$ x 10$\frac{7}{32}$ x $\frac{15}{32}$in (349 x 260 x 12mm)
PANEL SIDES	2 @ 17$\frac{21}{64}$ x 6$\frac{13}{16}$ x $\frac{15}{32}$in (440 x 173 x 12mm)
PANEL FRONT	1 @ 12$\frac{3}{16}$ x 7$\frac{3}{32}$ x $\frac{15}{32}$in (310 x 180 x 12mm)
PANEL REAR	1 @ 15½ x 5$\frac{5}{16}$ x $\frac{15}{32}$in (394 x 135 x 12mm)
FRONT INFILL	2 @ 3$\frac{15}{16}$ x 3¾ x ¾in (100 x 95 x 19mm)
REAR INFILL	2 @ 4$\frac{17}{32}$ x 3¾ x ¾in (115 x 95 x 19mm)
LEG INFILL	2 @ 6$\frac{19}{32}$ x 2$\frac{11}{64}$ x ¾in (168 x 55 x 19mm)
SUPPORT BATTENS	2 @ 10$\frac{7}{32}$ x ¾ x ¾in (260 x 19 x 19mm)

1 Using 1¾ x ¾in (44 x 19mm) prepared pine (*Pinus* spp.), cut the lengths for the wheelbarrow mainframe struts. The joining struts are cut at an angle of 7.5°. Make a template for the handle shape, and use this to mark the handle ends of the mainframe strut.

2 Cut out the shape using a bandsaw. Round over the contours for a smooth shape.

3 Cut out the blanks for the barrow using ½in (12mm) WBP plywood. Cut the required bevels to the bottom of the side panels.

4 The barrow base requires a tapered shape with bevels along the sides. A temporary spacer will allow the taper, and the bevel, to be cut with a bench saw. Alternatively, a jigsaw or circular saw could be used, with a guide.

5 The required bevels and angles are cut to the ends of the side panels. Make sure all the required bevels are cut, before marking and cutting the top edges of the panels.

6 Make and use a template to mark the shapes on the side, front and rear panels of the barrow.

7 Cut out the shapes using a bandsaw or jigsaw, sand the sawn edges to remove imperfections and sharp edges. Fill in any edge voids with filler.

8 Start assembling the barrow by first attaching the front and rear panels to the base panel, using screws and adhesive. I used ⅛ x 1⅛in (3 x 30mm) screws, into piloted holes.

9 Attach the side panels to the base, and front and rear panels using screws and adhesive.

10 Fill the countersunk holes to cover the screw heads.

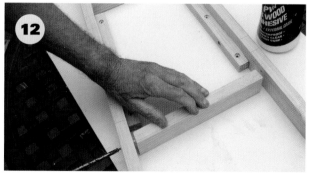

11 Start assembling the main frame by attaching the barrow attaching battens to the main frame side struts, using screws and adhesive.

12 Screw the crosspieces in place, again using glue to strengthen the fixing.

13 Check the angle of the sides for fitting the legs.

14 Mark the shape for the leg decorative infills, and cut out using a bandsaw or jigsaw. Attach each infill to the mainframe strut about midpoint of the leg position, with a size 20 jointing biscuit and adhesive.

15 The legs and decorative side supports are formed using 1¼ x 1¼in (33 x 33mm) pine. Cut the required lengths, and glue the short sections to the longer ones. Use a sliding bevel to check the required angle for the top of the leg and decorative support. Set

and cut the required angle using a mitre saw or bandsaw, on leg and side supports (the holding clamp has been removed in the picture above, for clarity).

16 The next step is to check the result in situ.

17 Cut out the remainder of the leg and side support shape using a bandsaw.

18 Drill and counter-bore the clearance holes for the attaching screws. Use the offcut wedge for support.

19 Cut the blanks for the front and rear decorative infills, for the required bevels and angles. Make a template and mark and cut out the decorative design.

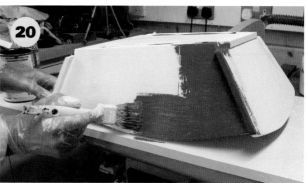

20 Apply primer, undercoat and top coat to all the surfaces, use masking tape to cover the surfaces that will be joined using adhesive.

21 Start final assembly by joining the mainframe to the bottom of the barrow, using screws through the attaching battens with added adhesive.

22 Attach each leg to the mainframe and the barrow sides, using screws and adhesive. There is also an additional screw through the decorative leg infill into the leg.

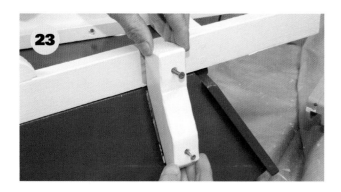

23 Next you need to attach the decorative side supports, with screws and adhesive.

24 Attach the front and rear decorative infills using screws and adhesive. You will need to slightly notch the corner of each infill to give clearance for the barrow base edge.

25 The wheel is carried using two spindle supports. These are cut to give an inner angle of 7.5°. Bore a ⅝in (15mm) hole ¾in (20mm) deep. Use a wedge offcut to assist drilling.

26 Cut two 1⅝in (40mm) lengths of ⅝in (15mm) copper pipe, then insert one into each spindle support to act as a bearing.

27 Feed a 5½in (140mm) length of ½in (12mm) studding through the wheel bore, and tighten centrally using ½in (12mm) washers and nuts, either side of the wheel. Feed each spindle support to the spindle ends.

28 Attach the spindle supports to the bottom front of the mainframe using screws. Check the wheel runs freely.

29 Scribe the true angle of the leg feet, and cut. Your finished wheelbarrow is ready for action.

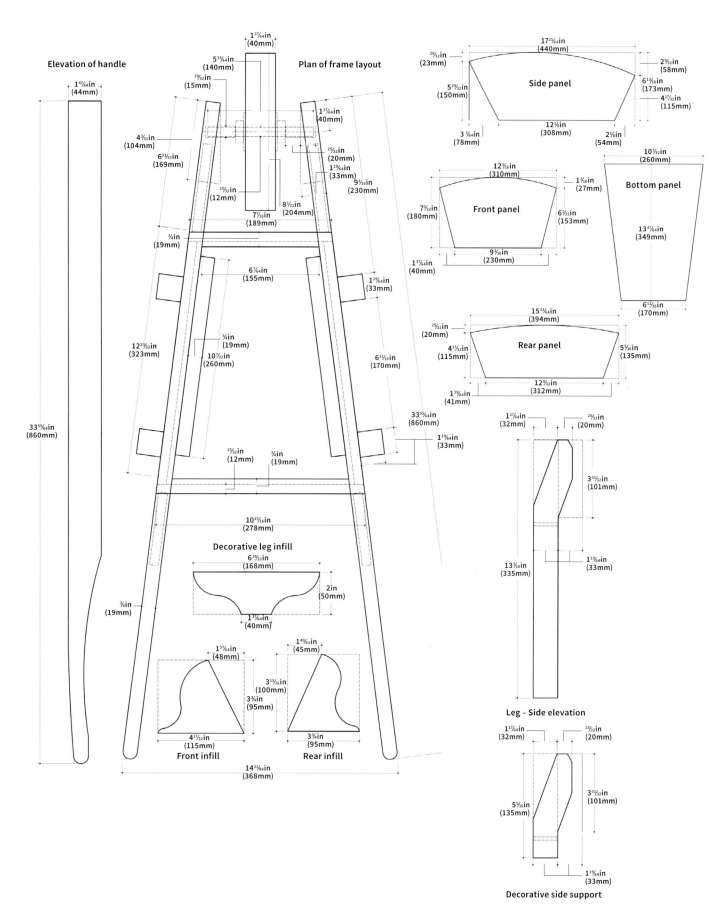

Elevation of handle

1⁴⁷⁄₆₄in
(44mm)

33⁵⁄₆₄in
(860mm)

¾in
(19mm)

Plan of frame layout

1³⁷⁄₆₄in
(40mm)

5³³⁄₆₄in
(140mm)

¹⁹⁄₃₂in
(15mm)

4³⁄₃₂in
(104mm)

6²¹⁄₃₂in
(169mm)

¹⁵⁄₃₂in
(12mm)

7⁷⁄₁₆in
(189mm)

1³⁷⁄₆₄in
(40mm)

²⁵⁄₃₂in
(20mm)

1¹⁹⁄₆₄in
(33mm)

9¹⁄₁₆in
(230mm)

8¹⁄₃₂in
(204mm)

¾in
(19mm)

6⁷⁄₆₄in
(155mm)

1¹⁹⁄₆₄in
(33mm)

12²³⁄₃₂in
(323mm)

¾in
(19mm)

10⁷⁄₃₂in
(260mm)

6¹¹⁄₁₆in
(170mm)

33⁵⁵⁄₆₄in
(860mm)

¹⁵⁄₃₂in
(12mm)

¾in
(19mm)

1¹⁹⁄₆₄in
(33mm)

10¹⁵⁄₁₆in
(278mm)

Decorative leg infill

6¹⁹⁄₃₂in
(168mm)

2in
(50mm)

1³⁷⁄₆₄in
(40mm)

¾in
(19mm)

14³¹⁄₆₄in
(368mm)

1⁵⁷⁄₆₄in
(48mm)

3¹⁵⁄₁₆in
(100mm)

3¾in
(95mm)

4¹¹⁄₃₂in
(115mm)

Front infill

1⁴⁹⁄₆₄in
(45mm)

3¾in
(95mm)

Rear infill

Side panel

17²¹⁄₆₄in
(440mm)

²⁹⁄₃₂in
(23mm)

2²⁵⁄₃₂in
(58mm)

6¹³⁄₁₆in
(173mm)

4¹⁷⁄₃₂in
(115mm)

5²⁹⁄₃₂in
(150mm)

3 ⁵⁄₆₄in
(78mm)

12¹⁄₈in
(308mm)

2⅛in
(54mm)

Front panel

12³⁄₁₆in
(310mm)

1¹⁄₁₆in
(27mm)

7³⁄₃₂in
(180mm)

6¹⁄₃₂in
(153mm)

1³⁷⁄₆₄in
(40mm)

9¹⁄₁₆in
(230mm)

Bottom panel

10⁷⁄₃₂in
(260mm)

13⁴⁷⁄₆₄in
(349mm)

6¹¹⁄₁₆in
(170mm)

Rear panel

15³³⁄₆₄in
(394mm)

²⁵⁄₃₂in
(20mm)

5⁵⁄₁₆in
(135mm)

4¹⁷⁄₃₂in
(115mm)

1³⁹⁄₆₄in
(41mm)

12²⁵⁄₃₂in
(312mm)

1¹⁷⁄₆₄in
(32mm)

²⁵⁄₃₂in
(20mm)

3³¹⁄₃₂in
(101mm)

13³⁄₁₆in
(335mm)

1¹⁹⁄₆₄in
(33mm)

Leg – Side elevation

1¹⁷⁄₆₄in
(32mm)

²⁵⁄₃₂in
(20mm)

3³¹⁄₃₂in
(101mm)

5⁵⁄₁₆in
(135mm)

1¹⁹⁄₆₄in
(33mm)

Decorative side support

MICRO SHED

Alan Holtham builds this small shed, perfect for storing garden tools

Cutting list

POSTS	4 @ 65²³⁄₆₄ x 2¾ x 2¾in
	(1660 x 70 x 70mm)
ROOF	2 @ 35⁵³⁄₆₄ x 32³²⁄₃₂ x 1in
	(910 x 820 x 25mm)
BARGE BOARD	4 @ 37⁵¹⁄₆₄ x 2¾ x ¹⁹⁄₃₂in
	(960 x 70 x 15mm)
FLOOR	1 @ 38⁷⁄₆₄ x 23¹⁵⁄₆₄ x ⁷⁄₁₆in
	(968 x 590 x 11mm)
FLOOR FRAME	2 @ 38⁷⁄₆₄ x 1⁴⁹⁄₆₄ x 1¹⁷⁄₆₄in
	(968 x 45 x 32mm)
FLOOR FRAME	2 @ 20⁴⁵⁄₆₄ x 1⁴⁹⁄₆₄ x 1¹⁷⁄₆₄in
	(526 x 45 x 32mm)
FRONT/BACK FRAME	
UPRIGHTS	4 @ 55⁵⁄₁₆ x 1⁴⁹⁄₆₄ x 1⁴⁹⁄₆₄in
	(1405 x 45 x 45mm)
UPRIGHTS	5 @ 49¼ x 1⁴⁹⁄₆₄ x 1⁴⁹⁄₆₄in
	(1251 x 45 x 45mm)
UPRIGHTS	4 @ 12³⁄₃₂ x 1⁴⁹⁄₆₄ x 1⁴⁹⁄₆₄in
	(307 x 45 x 45mm)
ROOF SUPPORTS	4 @ 26⁷⁄₃₂ x 1⁴⁹⁄₆₄ x 1⁴⁹⁄₆₄in
	(666 x 45 x 45mm)
HORIZONTALS	4 @ 34⁹⁄₁₆ x 1⁴⁹⁄₆₄ x 1⁴⁹⁄₆₄in
	(878 x 45 x 45mm)
RIDGE	1 @ 23¹⁵⁄₆₄ x 1⁴⁹⁄₆₄ x 1⁴⁹⁄₆₄in
	(590 x 45 x 45mm)
SIDE FRAME	
UPRIGHTS	4 @ 50²⁵⁄₃₂ x 1⁴⁹⁄₆₄ x 1⁴⁹⁄₆₄in
	(1290 x 45 x 45mm)
HORIZONTALS	5 @ 19¹¹⁄₁₆ x 1⁴⁹⁄₆₄ x 1⁴⁹⁄₆₄in
	(500 x 45 x 45mm)
POST FEET	4 @ 3¹⁵⁄₁₆ x 3¹⁵⁄₁₆ x 2in
	(100 x 100 x 50mm)
CLADDING TO FIT	

No matter what size garden you have, there never seems to be enough storage for all those essential maintenance tools and equipment. A shed is usually the answer, but even the smallest conventional shed is probably too big for a lot of small gardens; on the other hand, the mini versions you can buy are usually too small and flimsy to be of much use.

This micro shed is designed as a compromise, being roomy enough for a small lawnmower and a few tools, along with plenty of shelving for pots and buckets as well as containers of fertilizer, seeds and all the other gardening paraphernalia that seems to accumulate.

I like the idea of getting it up off the ground on the four legs. Not only does the gap underneath provide you with storage for those things that need to be under cover but don't necessarily need to be inside the shed, but more importantly it prevents the base sitting in the damp. This is always the first area to rot and unless you use top-quality timber it starts to deteriorate surprisingly quickly. With the shed on legs like this the air is free to circulate and only the bottom of the legs can rot – if they do you can just chop a few inches off! Yet another advantage is that it also discourages vermin – every shed I have ever had has always had mice nesting underneath.

This design makes it very easy to build. It's just four panels screwed together onto the legs, and you can scale it bigger or smaller to suit your own location. Whatever the size, it is worth paying a bit extra for decent quality materials. I used PAR redwood, which is about 15% more than the whitewood equivalent, but is far less knotty and the pieces are much straighter and squarer, which makes the construction easier.

1. All the material is standard off-the-shelf sections: 2¾ x 2¾in (70 x 70mm) for the legs, 1 ¾ x 1¾in (45 x 45mm) and 1¾ x 1¼in (45 x 32mm) for the framing, and shiplap cladding. Larger sections often have splits and cracks on the ends, so check these carefully and cut back to sound material. This is particularly important for the legs as they will soon start to deteriorate if water can get in. Cut the first leg to size and then use that as a template to mark out the others. You will need a 45° angle on one end of each leg.

   Next cut out all the pieces for the frames, cutting the longest lengths first then progressively smaller pieces from the remaining offcuts.

2 The frames are all screwed together and you can save yourself a lot of time by using a combined drill and countersink bit.

3 To assemble the joints accurately work on a clean, flat surface and use clamps to hold everything flush if need be. This is particularly useful when you screw the ridge piece joint together as the two mitres tend to slide against each other as you tighten up the screws.

4 Cut a temporary spacer to save measuring for the position of each of the internal uprights.

5 One central upright should be enough on the back panel, but I added two more as fixing supports for the slotted shelving I want to use when I fit the shed out.

6 The roof apex screws into place between the ends of the side uprights.

7 The completed back frame with a couple of additional strengtheners in the ridge section.

8 The side frames are made up in exactly the same way. Again, use the first one as a template for the other to make sure they are identical.

9 For speed, cut the cladding in batches leaving it approximately ⅛in (3mm) overlength. Check it over carefully first and discard any with loose knots.

10 The bottom one must be aligned carefully as all the others will follow off it. Leave approximately ¼in (6mm) overhang at the bottom to allow water to drip clear. Note the small amount of overhang at each end as well. Use plenty of nails to secure the bottom one, but then only one nail through the bottom of each piece of cladding for each subsequent one. Nailing this way will hold the top

of the cladding in place but still allow the wood to move with changes in humidity. If you nail them too tight the cladding will try and shrink and then split in the summer.

11 Mark the cladding up the ridge apex and cut roughly to size with a jigsaw.

12 Now you can run a bearing guided cutter around the outside of the frame to trim the overhanging cladding back. Remember to work anti-clockwise around the outside of a frame.

13 This should leave a perfect flush edge – so much easier than trying to cut and fix each piece individually.

14 Use up the short offcuts of cladding for the narrow sections either side of the doors. Trim these back with the router in the same way, but this time work clockwise around the internal opening.

15 If you leave plenty of spare when you jigsaw out the cladding for the openings, the subsequent

trimming cut with the router should produce a neat rounded corner. Repeat the same procedure for the two side panels, but check the path of the router carefully to ensure that the cutter bearing can't drop into a screw hole or you will get a neatly cut-out radius in your nice straight edge!

16 Use a small radius cutter to round the three exposed edges of the legs. This looks neat and minimizes the risk of chipping later.

17 Remember that these legs are 'handed', so mark the relevant ones before you start. The internal corner needs to be left square to butt the frames against.

18 The legs can now be screwed to the front and back frames. You will have to angle the screws slightly to clear the uprights.

19 The easiest way to assemble the shed is to lay the heavy back panel on the floor and attach the sides first.

20 Next drop the lighter front panel on top and screw through from underneath.

21 Now you can stand it up as one piece, but make sure the legs can't slide away backwards as you lift; as I work on my own, I used some heavy weights as 'backstops'.

22 The doors use the same frame and cladding construction, so make up the two frame first in the same way as the other panels.

23 I changed my mind on these and decided to cover them with vertical tongues and grooves rather than shiplap. Hold the boards tight together with a clamp and nail on as before.

24 If you centralize the boards on the frame and then cut an even amount off either side it looks better than having one narrow piece on one side, but leave a good amount of overhang to ensure a weatherproof seal when the doors are closed.

25 I finished them off by running a 45° chamfer bit all round to leave an edge that matched the V groove on the boards.

26 Yet another frame is needed for the base; put in a couple of cross bearers to support the plywood floor.

27 This frame is screwed into the base of the shed, but drop it down ½in (12mm) so that the ply base ends up flush with the top of the frame section.

28 The easiest way to cut up ply sheets is to use a circular saw on a track; you should be able to get them to a perfect finished size in this way.

29 The base should then drop in place and you can either nail or screw it in place, depending on whether you ever anticipate dismantling the shed again to move it.

30 The front and back apexes are tied together with a piece of 2 x 2in (50 x 50mm) screwed through from either end.

THE ROOF

31 I used 1in (25mm) exterior ply for the roof, which was really a bit too heavy – ¾in (18mm) would probably suffice, but even that would still be awkward to hold, so use clamps as temporary supports.

32 Ideally, you should cut a 45° chamfer on the top edges so that they butt together on the apex and then screw the ply in place. This will be covered with felt shingles when the shed is reassembled on site.

33 Barge boards on the front are not essential, but they do leave a better finished appearance as they cover the exposed ply and the felt edges.

34 I prefer to use galvanized hinges, as they don't rust like the black japanned ones always seem to do.

35 Because of the way the doors sit off the front of the shed you will need to fit a packing strip behind them the same thickness as that of the doors.

36 A thin strip glued and pinned onto one of the doors covers the gap when they are shut. Leave a good gap here, something like ⅛in (3mm), to make sure the doors don't bind during wet weather.

37 Small hardwood feet keep the ends of the softwood legs clear of the wet ground and will prolong their life considerably.

38 The finished shed with a strong bolt to keep the first door closed and a heavy-duty lockable hasp/bolt. Choose a suitable weatherproof finish and give the shed two coats for plenty of protection. When reassembled on site, add felt shingles to the roof.

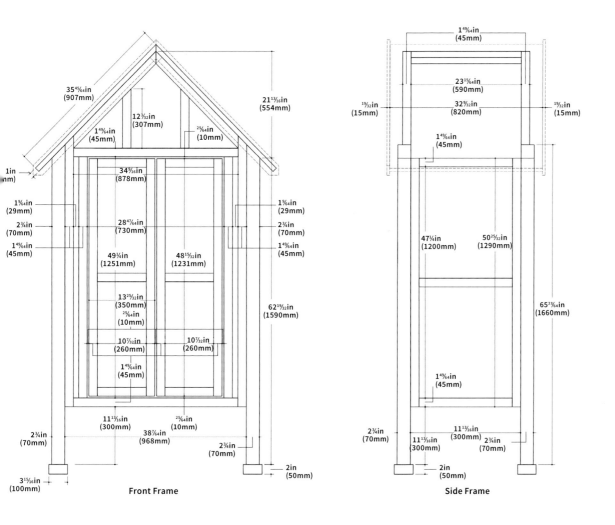

Front Frame

Side Frame

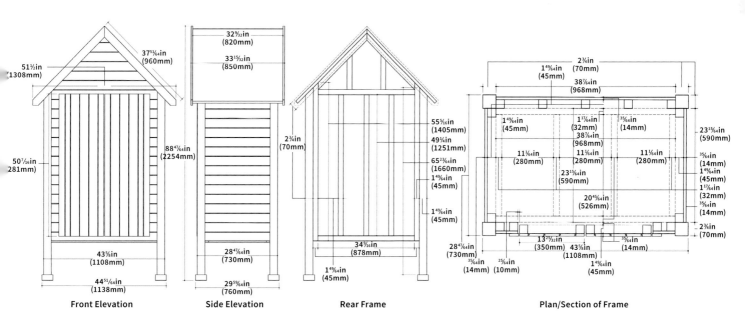

Front Elevation

Side Elevation

Rear Frame

Plan/Section of Frame

DECKCHAIR

Soak up the sun with Simon Rodway's sturdy take on the folding deckchair

The deckchair used to summon up images of the seafront – lines of holidaymakers on the beach, baking or freezing in the great British summer. Although they have survived practically unaltered for at least half a century, I've never found them that comfortable, due to the lack of back support; so I've come up with something a bit more substantial. In fact, it probably owes a bit more to the traditional steamer chair that used to adorn the decks of passenger ships, but with a more contemporary feel.

Cutting list

BACK LEGS	2 @ Ex 32¼ x 6¹¹⁄₁₆ x ¾in (820 x 170 x 20mm)
FRONT LEGS	2 @ Ex 41⅜ x 7¹⁵⁄₃₂ x ¾in (1050 x 190 x 20mm)
BACK SLATS	8 @ 21⅞ x 1¾ x ¾in (555 x 44 x 20mm)
BACK SLATS	1 @ 21⅞ x 2⅝ x ¾in (555 x 64 x 20mm)
SEAT SLATS	6 @ 19⁵⁄₁₆ x 1¾ x ¾in (490 x 44 x 20mm)
SEAT SLATS	8 @ 19⁵⁄₁₆ x 2⅝ x ¾in (490 x 64 x 20mm)

FRONT BRACE	1 @ 21⅞ x 1¼ x ¾in (555 x 33 x 20mm)
BACK BRACE	1 @ 19⁵⁄₁₆ x 1⅜ x ¾in (490 x 33 x 20mm)
TURNED CAPS	4 @ 2in (50mm) diameter x ½in (13mm)
SPACERS	2 @ 2in (50mm) diameter x ½in (13mm)
STEEL BOLTS & LOCK NUTS	2 @ ¼in (8mm) diameter to fit

You will need to start with the legs, by making a template for each. I am going to refer to the front and back legs, although one also supports the seat, the other the back – hopefully it won't be too confusing. The best way to go with the wood on this project is to use hardwood. You will need to source some reasonably wide planks to cut the leg shapes from.

Once you have cut out the legs, clamp them together as front and back pairs and drill matching pilot holes through each pair to mark the pivot point of the bolts. Using the angle formed by the intersection of the seat support edge, and the back edge, transfer this to your bottom – wider – back slat. This slat will form the stop against the back legs, so it is important that the chamfer along the bottom edge sits cleanly on the top of the legs. Also mark the position of the cut you will make to let the bottom slat in at this point.

To do this you will also need to mark and cut the dovetail angle on the upper edge of this slat, and then mark out and cut dovetail shaped tenons on the ends of all the other back slats, to the same depth – shown as ¾in (20mm) – as your front legs. The dovetail ends are designed to lock the back slats into the back to make your deckchair rigid. Glue and screw the pair of front legs together, and then do the same with the back legs, having

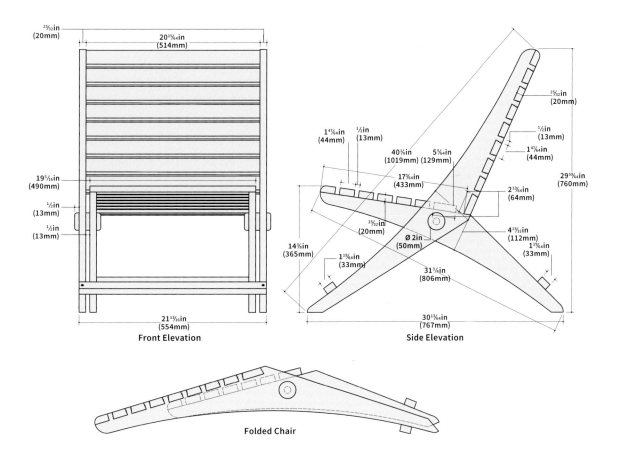

Front Elevation

Side Elevation

Folded Chair

rounded over the two end slats in each case. The seat slats just sit on top of the legs. Slide the seat/back legs inside the front legs and using the pilot holes as guides, check the alignment. When you are happy that they sit properly, and also close, drill the ⁵⁄₁₆in (8mm) holes for the steel bolts, which are secured with locking nuts. This is obviously easier to do when the pairs of legs are clamped together, but leaving it until now allows some last minute adjustment to the location of the pivot centre.

I have shown a ½in (13mm) wood spacer between the legs on each side, with timber caps glued to the inner and outer legs as covers for the bolt ends. The spacer helps the folding process, and makes it less hazardous for fingers as well. You may need to sand these down a little during fitting so that the legs pivot properly. Then fit the bottom braces front and back, and your deckchair is complete.

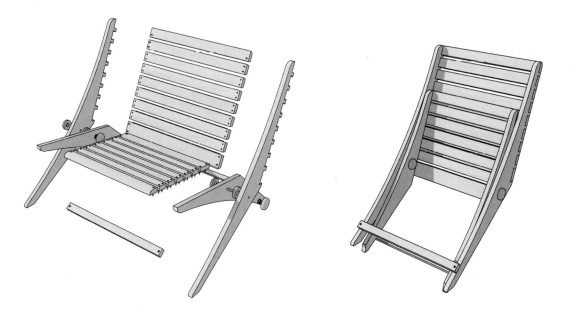

NESTING BOX

Make this wonderful nesting box and you can watch the birdies

What you need

- 15mm exterior-grade ply
- Softwood batten
- 1in to 1¼in (25 to 32mm) drill bit
- Brass or plastic hinges
- ½ and 2in (12.5 and 50mm) screws
- Plastic wall plugs
- Panel pins

Everyone needs a home and that includes our feathered friends. Enjoy watching their development and their antics with this great bird box.

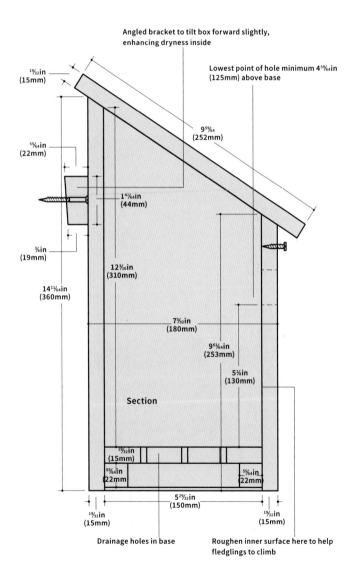

Angled bracket to tilt box forward slightly, enhancing dryness inside

Lowest point of hole minimum 4⁵⁄₆₄in (125mm) above base

¹⁹⁄₃₂in (15mm)

⁵⁵⁄₆₄in (22mm)

9⁵⁄₆₄in (252mm)

1⁴⁄₆₄in (44mm)

¾in (19mm)

12³⁄₁₆in (310mm)

14¹¹⁄₆₄in (360mm)

7³⁄₃₂in (180mm)

9⁶¹⁄₆₄in (253mm)

5⅛in (130mm)

Section

¹⁹⁄₃₂in (15mm)

⁵⁵⁄₆₄in (22mm)

⁵⁵⁄₆₄in (22mm)

5²⁹⁄₃₂in (150mm)

¹⁹⁄₃₂in (15mm)

¹⁹⁄₃₂in (15mm)

Drainage holes in base

Roughen inner surface here to help fledglings to climb

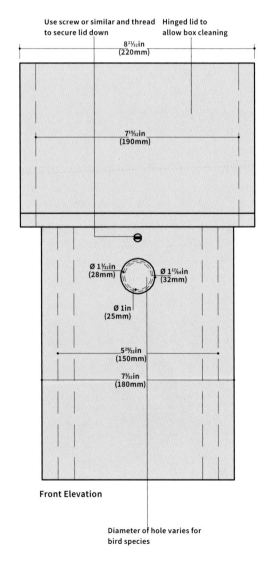

Use screw or similar and thread to secure lid down

Hinged lid to allow box cleaning

8²¹⁄₃₂in (220mm)

7¹⁵⁄₃₂in (190mm)

Ø 1¹⁄₃₂in (28mm)

Ø 1¹¹⁄₆₄in (32mm)

Ø 1in (25mm)

5²⁹⁄₃₂in (150mm)

7³⁄₃₂in (180mm)

Front Elevation

Diameter of hole varies for bird species

HOW TO MAKE IT

Cut out all the parts from ⅝in (15mm) ply as per the drawings. Ensure all edges are cut square, apart from the top edges of the back and front panels, which have a bevel cut to take the lid.

The bottom board has small holes to help keep the nest dry inside. The entry hole can be anywhere between 1 and 1¼in (25–32mm) in diameter, depending on what spade bits you have and what species of bird you want to attract to the nesting box. Blue, coal and marsh tits need a 1in (25mm) hole. For great tits, tree sparrows and pied flycatchers it is 1⅛in (28mm), and for house sparrows and nuthatches it is 1¼in (32mm).

The batten is fixed to the birdbox before fixing the whole thing to the wall – this allows the lid to hinge back properly. There is a screw on the front around which a simple metal loop hooks to keep it closed.

Use a non-toxic exterior wood finish for the safety of the birds, and to avoid putting them off because of vapour smells. A nice quick project that will bring life to your garden or backyard.

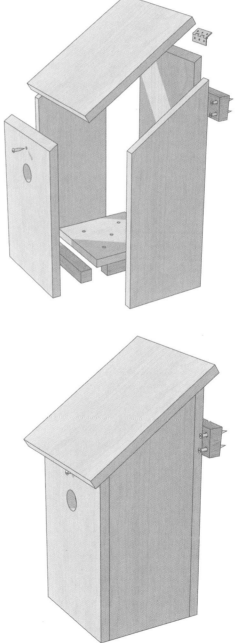

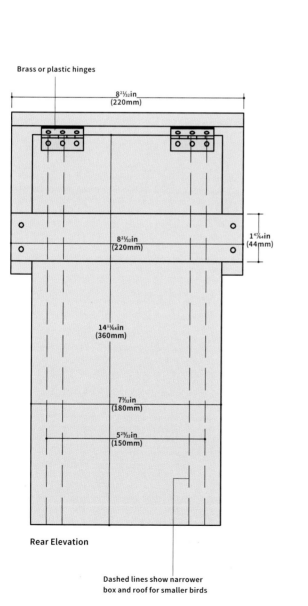

Brass or plastic hinges

8²¹⁄₃₂in (220mm)

8²¹⁄₃₂in (220mm)

1⁴⁷⁄₆₄in (44mm)

14¹⁵⁄₆₄in (360mm)

7³⁄₃₂in (180mm)

5²⁹⁄₃₂in (150mm)

Rear Elevation

Dashed lines show narrower box and roof for smaller birds

GARDEN ARBOUR

This lovely piece of garden furniture will add a touch of charm to any garden

What you need

- ¾ x ¾in (75 x 75mm) treated softwood posts
- 4 x 1in (100 x 25mm) treated sawn softwood
- 2 x 1in (50 x 25mm) treated sawn softwood
- Pre-assembled diamond trellis panels
- 2 and 3in (50mm and 75mm) exterior grade decking screws
- 2in (50mm) galvanized nails
- Coloured garden finish
- Hardpoint saw or mitre saw

This project looks more complicated than it really is. For a start, although we have given dimensions, you will want to resize it to suit the trellis panel sizes you can get hold of, which you can buy from many timber merchants, fencing suppliers or garden centres.

HOW TO MAKE IT

Cut the posts to length, bearing in mind the method you will use to hold the arbour in the ground. To fix it securely, I would use short metal posts braces pushed into the ground, possibly with stone or concrete slabs under the seat, as it is easier to maintain and resist foot wear. Screw (or nail) the trellis panels between the posts after

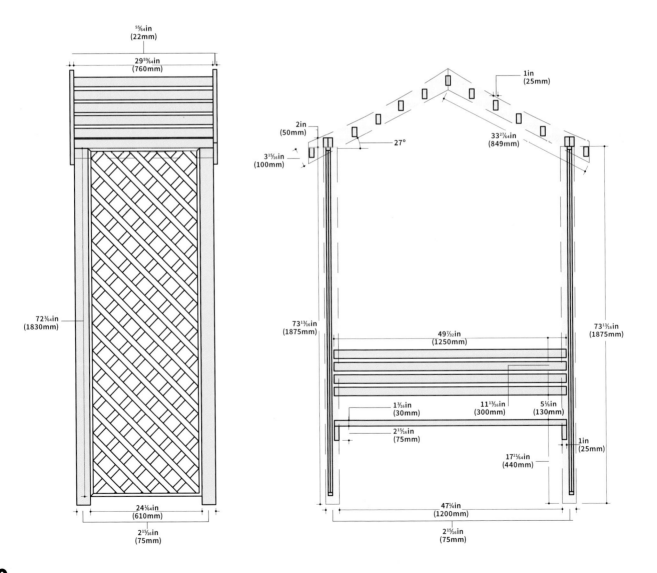

notching out for the lower rails. Screw the lower rails in place and then cut and screw the back rails, after first checking the posts are parallel, then fit the seat rails.

The two roof sections are assembled separately on the workbench with the cross rails set at the same matching angle as the ends of the front and back boards; do this using exterior grade screws.

Note how two battens are screwed together in line with where the vertical posts will come.

The two roof sections need to be plated together (not shown) using two pieces of 4 x 2in (100 x 50mm) softwood running crosswise on the outer faces of the front and back roof boards.

Having done the full assembly with assistance, lay it down and hammer on the metposts, then raise it to the vertical. Use a sledgehammer and sacrificial block to fix the structure in place, taking care not to damage the posts. Keep them vertical, working around all four repeatedly, until it sits correctly. Now lift the slatted roof into position and use some long screws to fasten down onto the posts. Lastly, apply a finish such as a water-based garden paint, in the colour you desire. Time to break out the wine and drink a toast to the long hot summer the arbour deserves.

ADIRONDACK LOVESEAT

This stylish Adirondack seat designed by Simon Rodway and built by Alan Goodsell will add charm to any outside space

Cutting list

BACK LEGS	3 @ Ex 37⅜ x 4¾ x ¾in (950 x 119 x 20mm)	BACK RAIL	1 @ Ex 55 x 2¾ x 1¾in (1400 x 69 x 44mm)
BACK SLATS	14 @ 36½ x 3¾ x ¾in (900 x 96 x 20mm)	SEAT SLATS	12 @ 49⅝ x 1¾ x ¾in (1260 x 44 x 20mm)
BACK INFILL	2 @ 28⅜ x 2¾ x ¾in (720 x 69 x 20mm)	FRONT LEGS	2 @ 20⅞ x 3¾ x 1¾in (530 x 96 x 44mm)
SEAT/BOTTOM RAILS	2 @ 49⅝ x 2¾ x ¾in (1260 x 69 x 20mm)	ARM BRACES	2 @ 15 x 2¾ x ¾in (380 x 69 x 20mm)
ARMS	2 @ Ex 29⅜ x 5¹¹⁄₁₆ x ¾in (750 x 144 x 20mm)	BACK SLAT BRACES	2 @ Ex 25⅝ x 2¾ x ¾in (650 x 69 x 20mm)

The loveseat was not, as its name implies, originally for amorous purposes at all, but was a wider chair designed in the early 18th-century to accommodate the dresses worn by fashionable ladies. However, a century later the wide chair had become a small two-seater sofa and acquired its name of loveseat or courting chair. For this project, an outdoor version was chosen, based on a classic American design, the Adirondack chair. The overall shape and geometry of the Adirondack chair is determined principally by the back leg, which also provides support for the seat slats, and the back is a fan shape of vertical slats, usually between four and seven to a chair. There are almost no joints, unless you count the odd notch and, in this case, a half-lap so the tool requirement here is pretty minimal. The wood sizes are standard joinery section sizes and ¾in (20mm) wood is used throughout, with the exception of the front legs and the back support rail, which are both 44mm (1¾in) thick.

1 Like any woodworking project the first step is to get together all the components you will need and machine them to size. I used rough-sawn wood, dimensioned it on the table saw and then planed it to a finish on a planer and thicknesser.

2 Use a cutoff saw to cut the components to length.

Mark the rough-sawn wood to lengths – it is a good idea to write what the components are on the wood.

3 Lay out all the pieces ready for planning.

4 Use a planer to machine the first surfaces.

5 Feed the pieces through the thicknesser to get them to their final dimension.

FRAME ASSEMBLY

The first thing to do is establish the shape of the back legs, of which there are three, one at each end and one in the middle. Cut an angled section from the back at 18°; this is effectively the back foot as it's the part that sits on the ground. Add the notch for the back seat rail; this will be cut out from what is going to be the top of the leg, and is angled at 3° to the top edge.

The remaining shaping of the leg is critical, not in terms of the geometry, but for comfort and appearance. The dished curve for the seat is about ¾in (20mm) at its deepest and then thickens slightly at the front end, where a series of 1¾in (44mm) long angled cuts are shown to allow snug fixing of the slats here so that they wrap nicely around the front of the seat. Once you're happy with the back legs, you can fix the bottom rail and slats to them.

Both rail and slats are all the same length as the seat rail at 49⅝in (1260mm). Apart from the front four seat slats, which are as close together as possible, I gave a spacing of about ¼in (6mm) between all other slats. These are rounded over along the top edges. The position of the bottom rail is located so that the front leg will hide the end grain when it's fixed in place. Cut and shape the front legs, arm braces and arms next, and fix the front legs in place so that they cover the ends of the bottom rails and the back feet sit flush with the ground. Secure the front legs firmly to the back legs with screws, and then cut and taper the vertical back slats, from 3½in (90mm) wide at the top to 2⅜in (60mm) at the bottom.

Turning to the seat rail next, cut to length and add the dishing or cutout on each side which will give the seat backs a slight curve. Some Adirondack chair designs leave the back flat and this is an easier option to build, but I think it adds to the comfort and appearance of your loveseat to add a small curve here. I have suggested a cutout of about ¾in (19mm) deep and just under 17¾in (450mm) wide for each side, with only the four outer slats each side angled, leaving the middle three set back but flat. This is really something you can experiment with, and maybe sacrifice a trial rail to getting it right. At the same time, establish the positions and spacing of the back slats, but leave the final fixing of these for the moment.

6 Cut the angles for the three first seat slats on the front ends of the back legs.

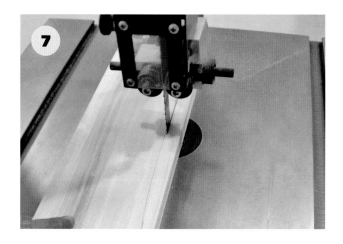

7 Mark and cut the curves on the back legs.

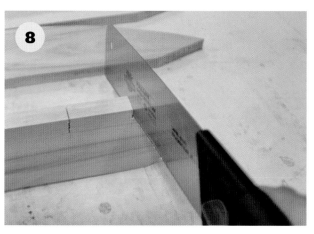

8 Mark and hand-cut the notches in the back legs for the seat rail.

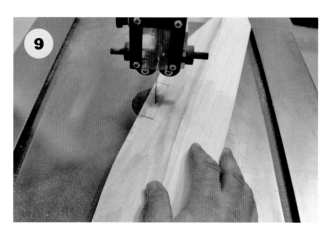

9 Finish cutting the notches with a bandsaw.

10 Mark and cut the arms to shape.

11 Set up the router table to cut the roundovers on the seat slats.

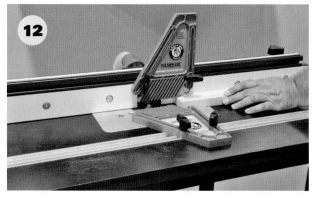

12 Proceed to cut the roundovers on all the upper surfaces of the seat slats; hold-downs make this safe and easy.

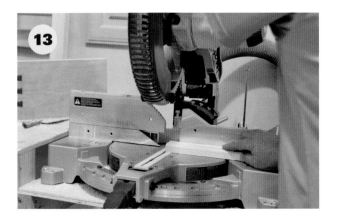

13 Square the ends of the seat slats.

14 Cut them to length.

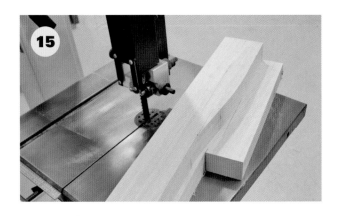

15 Mark and cut the front legs to shape, cut one then flip it over and mark the other from it to economize on wood.

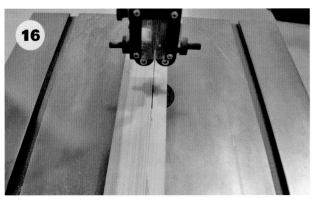

16 Cut the curve for the back slats in the seat rail.

17 Cut the angles on the back slats using a bandsaw then pass them over the planer to finish them.

18 Lay out the back slats on the seat rail and screw them at the bottom, then fan them out and mark and cut the curve on the tops.

BACK AND ASSEMBLY

With the slats in place, locate a centre point about 17in (430mm) down the centre line of the middle slat on each side, and draw a curve across the top of your slats using a trammel. Remove the slats and cut them out to form curves on each back, and re-fix to the seat rail. Next, fix the arms in place, provisionally with single screws, and offer up the back support, cut long, to the back and the arms. You can mark and cut the shoulders for the half lap on the ends of the back rail at this point, and then scribe the positions of the back slats on the top of the back rail, so that you can make angled cuts and end up with the rail flush against all slats. You will need to adjust the positions of the arms and back rail until you achieve a proper fit, and then finish the joint between them with screws each side, shaping the ends of the back rail to match the curve of the arms at the same time. Secure the arms firmly with multiple screws into the top of the front legs and the braces and put two screws through each back slat into the back rail. Optionally, fit small shaped braces across the back and above the back rail to stiffen the back slats, and finally, add the two infill pieces between the back slats to finish off your loveseat.

19 Position the back rail at the correct height and mark where it needs to be cut for the back slats.

20 Next screw the back slats to the back rail.

21 Screw the front legs to the outsides of the back legs. Next screw the outer legs to the bottom rail and screw the middle back leg to the rail exactly in the centre.

22 Screw the back assembly to the leg assembly so the arms can be fitted.

23 The shape cut into the seat and back rail makes a gentle curve for the seat back.

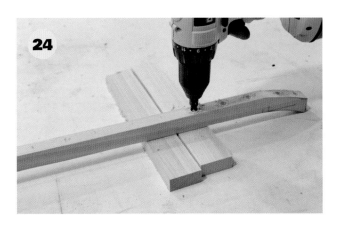

24 Cut and drill the back braces.

25 As with all the components at this stage, trial fit and screw the back braces to the back slats.

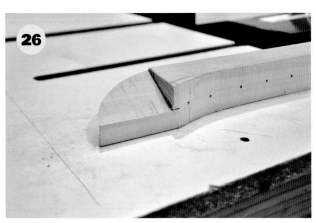

26 Cut the curve and angle for the arm ends on each end of the back rail.

27 Trial fit and screw the arms to the front legs and back rail.

28 Cut, fit and screw the infill pieces in place.

29 Screw the first three seat slats to the front of the back legs.

30 Using a spacer, screw the rest of the seat slats in place.

31 With all the seat slats screwed in place the chair is looking good.

32 Screw the arm braces in place.

33 The chair looks finished but it isn't – it all needs to come apart again for sanding.

34 Using a linisher, sand the curves smooth.

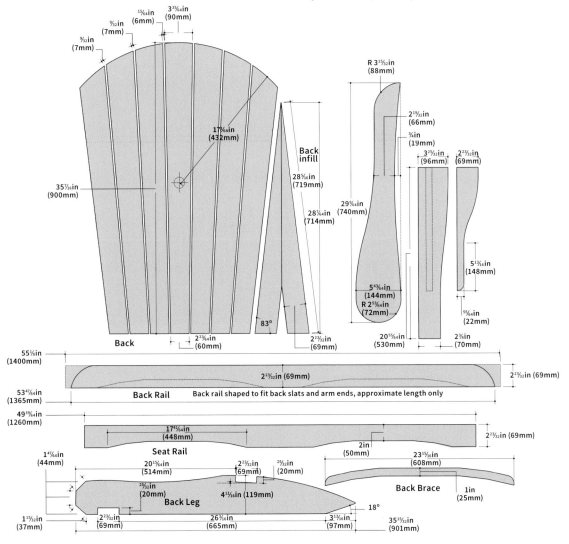

35 The arms get a roundover on their top surface.

36 All the components are sanded before reassembly. Screw the chair together, ready for the finish of your choice, either paint or oil.

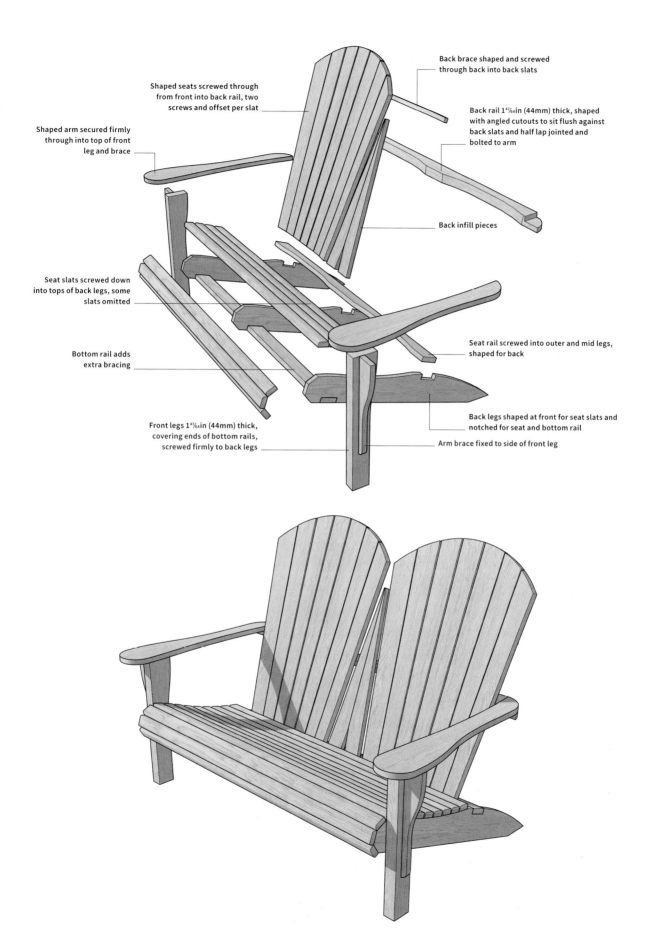

Back brace shaped and screwed through back into back slats

Shaped seats screwed through from front into back rail, two screws and offset per slat

Back rail 1⁴⁷⁄₆₄in (44mm) thick, shaped with angled cutouts to sit flush against back slats and half lap jointed and bolted to arm

Shaped arm secured firmly through into top of front leg and brace

Back infill pieces

Seat slats screwed down into tops of back legs, some slats omitted

Seat rail screwed into outer and mid legs, shaped for back

Bottom rail adds extra bracing

Back legs shaped at front for seat slats and notched for seat and bottom rail

Front legs 1⁴⁷⁄₆₄in (44mm) thick, covering ends of bottom rails, screwed firmly to back legs

Arm brace fixed to side of front leg

POTTING BENCH

This handy potting table by Alan Goodsell is a boon for any avid gardener

Cutting list

Table Base

FRONT AND BACK TOP RAILS	2 @ 48 X 3 X ¾in (1220 X 75 X 19mm)
FRONT LEGS LEFT AND RIGHT	2 @ 35¼in x 3 x 1½in (896 x 75 x 38mm)
SIDE RAILS TOP	2 @ 19 x 3 x ¾in (485 x 75 x 19mm)
SIDE RAILS BOTTOM	2 @ 16 x 3 x ¾in (405 x 75 x 19mm)
FRONT AND BACK BOTTOM RAILS	2 @ 41 x 3 x ¾in (1040 x 75 x 19mm)
LEFT AND RIGHT	2 @ 48 x 3 x 1½in (1220 x 75 x 38mm)
SIDE UPSTANDS	2 @ 20½ x 6 x ¾in (522 x 150 x 19mm)
BACK UPSTAND	1 @ 41 x 3 x ¾in (1040 x 75 x 19mm)

Shelf Unit

SIDES	30 x 8 x ¾in (760 x 200 x 19mm)
SHELF UPSTAND	1 @ 41 x 2 x ¾in (1040 x 50 x 19mm)
SHELVES	2 @ 41 x 7 x ¾in (1040 x 180 x 19mm)
TOP BACK	1 @ 41 x 6 x ¾in (1040 x 150 x 19mm)

Wheels and Axle

WHEELS	2 @ 8in (200mm) dia.
AXLE	1 @ ⁵/₁₆ x 24in (8 x 610mm)
NUTS	6 @ ⁵/₁₆in (8mm) thread
ACORN NUTS	2 @ ⁵/₁₆in (8mm) thread
WASHERS	8 to fit

This table is designed so it will be at home in any garden, large or small. For the smaller garden it can be used as an attractive plant display shelf as well as a place to do your potting. For the larger garden it is easily wheeled to any location to do your plant maintenance.

How to make it

There is nothing complicated about this project as it is simply components cut to size and screwed together, and if you want to make it really sturdy add some waterproof glue to the mating parts as they are assembled. The first thing to do is convert the pile of sawn wood – I used poplar – into components and then plane it all to size. This is done with the tablesaw, planer and thicknesser. If you don't have these tools you can buy the wood ready prepared as the sizes are pretty much standard, and if the wood you buy it sized slightly differently just make minor size adjustments.

When this it done, start cutting the components to length. The wheels and axle came from my local hardware store and you will be able to find something similar.

1 Cut the sawn wood into manageable pieces.

2 Plane the wood to make it smooth and square.

BASE UNIT

I decided to start with the lower frame and assemble the parts as I went, and then cut the next parts to length. Doing it this way will make sure that everything fits as you can measure the piece you have just made to get the exact measurements for the next part. Cut the four components to length and screw them together.

The slats are now attached to the frame. They have a rounded top edge to soften them, and this was done on the router table. Cut them to length, sand them and screw them in place on the frame. Conveniently, I found that a pencil was the right size to gap the slats and when they are attached the frame is nice and sturdy.

Make the top frame next, which consists of the long rails which are the long arms for the handle and the end rails which are screwed to them; these will be hidden by an upstand, so they need to be set in from the end to allow for this.

The next step is to add the legs. This is slightly tricky as they are all different lengths. Use the front right leg as the starting point and cut this one 35¼in (896mm) long, then cut the front left leg 2in (50mm) shorter to give clearance for the wheel; cut a radius on the end of this leg to give clearance when the table is tilted to move it. Now cut the back right leg; this one is 12¾in (324mm) longer than the front leg to give support to the shelf unit on the back. Lastly cut the back left leg; this one is 2in (50mm) shorter

than the right leg to allow for the wheel. Radius the end of this leg too. Cut notches for the top end rails to fit into; this makes the table easier to assemble. The ⁵⁄₁₆in (8mm) holes for the wheel spindle will be more accurate if done on the drill press before assembly.

Place the top frame on its side on a flat table and screw the back legs to it, spacer blocks are placed under the legs to keep them evenly spaced. Just use one screw per leg at this stage so the assembly can be adjusted for squareness when all the parts are together. Next place the lower frame onto the legs and screw that in place with one screw per leg. Turn the assembly over and screw the front legs to the assembly, then, using a builder's square make sure the table is square and screw all the rest of the screws into the legs.

The table can now be set on its feet. Slide the threaded axle through the wheels and legs at this stage; this is a temporary step to keep the table level while finishing off the top. Next cut the slats for the top; the two end slats are notched around the back legs and are also rounded on the top edges. Screw the two end slats in place and evenly space all the others between them, the pencils are used again. This is a good time to cut the dowel for the handle and screw it in place and also to screw an upstand to the back of the table's back legs.

3 Cut the pieces to length. It can be easier to cut two pieces at the same time to make sure they are exactly the same

4 Sand the parts before assembling.

5 Mark out the positions of screw holes then drill and countersink them.

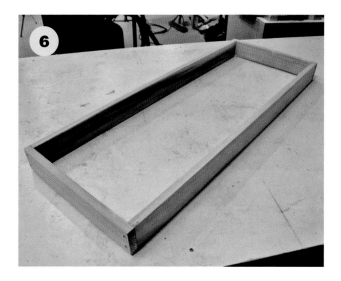

6 Screw the top frame together.

7 Round the top edges of the slats on the router table.

8 Make sure the frame is square.

9 Screw the slats to the frame spacing them evenly. Conveniently, a pencil worked for me this time.

10 The lower frame is now nice and sturdy.

11 Cut a radius on the ends of the legs with wheels.

12 Cut notches on the legs for the top end rails to fit into.

13 Mark and drill the holes for the dowel handle and also cut the radius on the end of the rail.

14 Screw the top frame together.

15 Drill the axle holes in the legs on the drill press.

16 Mark the position of the lower shelf on the legs.

17 Screw the top frame to the back legs, only use one screw at this stage.

18 Screw the lower frame to the back legs. Again, only use one screw.

19 Using a builder's square make sure the table is square, then screw in all the rest of the screws.

20 Put the table on the floor and temporarily add the wheels to make sure it is level.

21 Cut notches to the top slats to fit round the back legs.

22 Round over all the top slats' upper edges and fit the end two slats.

23 Position the slats and space them evenly. My pencil was useful for this again.

24 All the slats in place and the table is coming together.

25 Cut the dowel handle to length.

26 Attach the handle to the arms with screws.

27 Cut and screw the back upstand to the back of the legs. It was supposed to come to the edge of the legs, but I cut it a bit short. Hopefully nobody will notice!

SHELF UNIT

The shelf unit is made so it attaches to the long back legs and can be easily taken off to transport the table. The lower shelf sits on top of the back legs too. Mark and cut the notch in the back of the shelf uprights and round over the top front to give it a softer look. The shelves have an upstand and the lower one is just straight but the top one needs to be more decorative. I had a few ideas on this but chose a traditional heart shape. Mark and cut this out, sand and cut all the shelf parts to length and lay them on the table to see how they look. Next screw the upstands to the shelves and then screw them to the shelf unit uprights. This needs careful marking and drilling.

With the shelf unit made, it can be screwed to the table – three screws in each upright should do it – and the last piece of woodworking is to cut, fit and attach the end upstands.

The wheels and axle are bolted in place. Follow the photos to see how I positioned all the washers and bolts to keep everything locked together. To finish off, put an acorn nut on the end of the axle. The table can be finished to your taste, stained and oiled or painted. I used a product designed to protect and waterproof decks.

The final thing to do is gather your plants together and get potting.

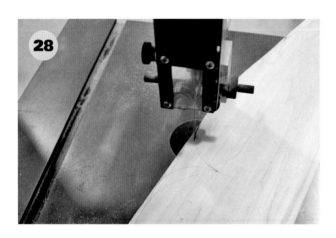

28 Cut the shelf sides and the top shelf back piece, use any design on the top that you like.

29 Lay out all the shelf components to make sure it looks right.

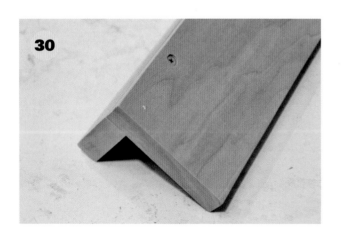

30 Screw the upstand to the lower shelf and repeat with the top shelf.

31 Screw the shelves to the sides.

32 Screw the shelf unit to the table's back legs.

33 Cut, fit and screw the side upstands to each end of the table.

34 The table is pretty much finished at this stage – just need to fit the wheels.

35 Arrange the bolts and washers like this and it will keep everything tight.

36 The acorn nut is a nice finishing touch.

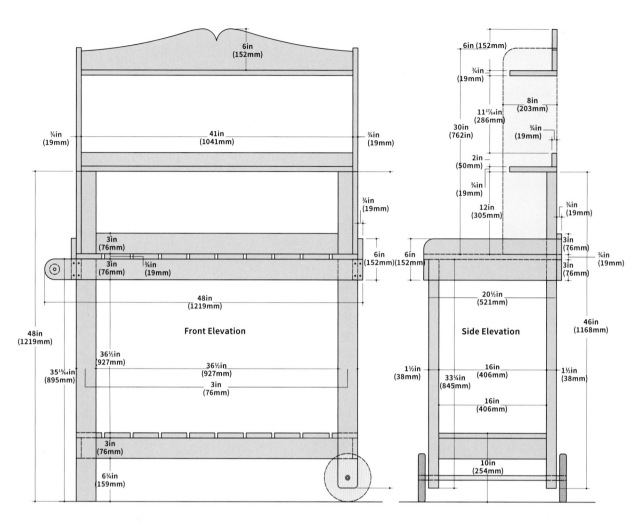

6in
(152mm)

¾in
(19mm)

41in
(1041mm)

¾in
(19mm)

¾in
(19mm)

3in
(76mm)

3in
(76mm)

¾in
(19mm)

6in
(152mm)

48in
(1219mm)

Front Elevation

48in
(1219mm)

36½in
(927mm)

36½in
(927mm)

3in
(76mm)

35¹⁵⁄₆₄in
(895mm)

6¼in
(159mm)

6in
(152mm)

¾in
(19mm)

8in
(203mm)

11¹⁷⁄₆₄in
(286mm)

30in
(762in)

¾in
(19mm)

2in
(50mm)

¾in
(19mm)

12in
(305mm)

¾in
(19mm)

3in
(76mm)

¾in
(19mm)

3in
(76mm)

6in
(152mm)

Side Elevation

20½in
(521mm)

46in
(1168mm)

1½in
(38mm)

33¼in
(845mm)

16in
(406mm)

1½in
(38mm)

16in
(406mm)

10in
(254mm)

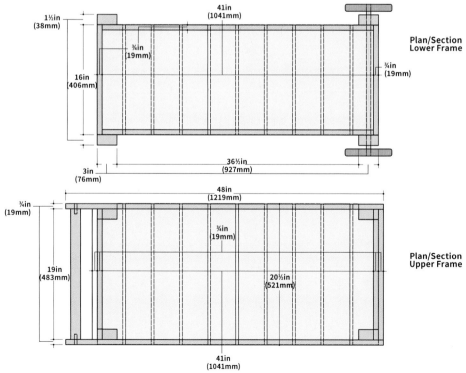

41in
(1041mm)

1½in
(38mm)

¾in
(19mm)

**Plan/Section
Lower Frame**

16in
(406mm)

¾in
(19mm)

36½in
(927mm)

3in
(76mm)

48in
(1219mm)

¾in
(19mm)

¾in
(19mm)

**Plan/Section
Upper Frame**

19in
(483mm)

20½in
(521mm)

41in
(1041mm)

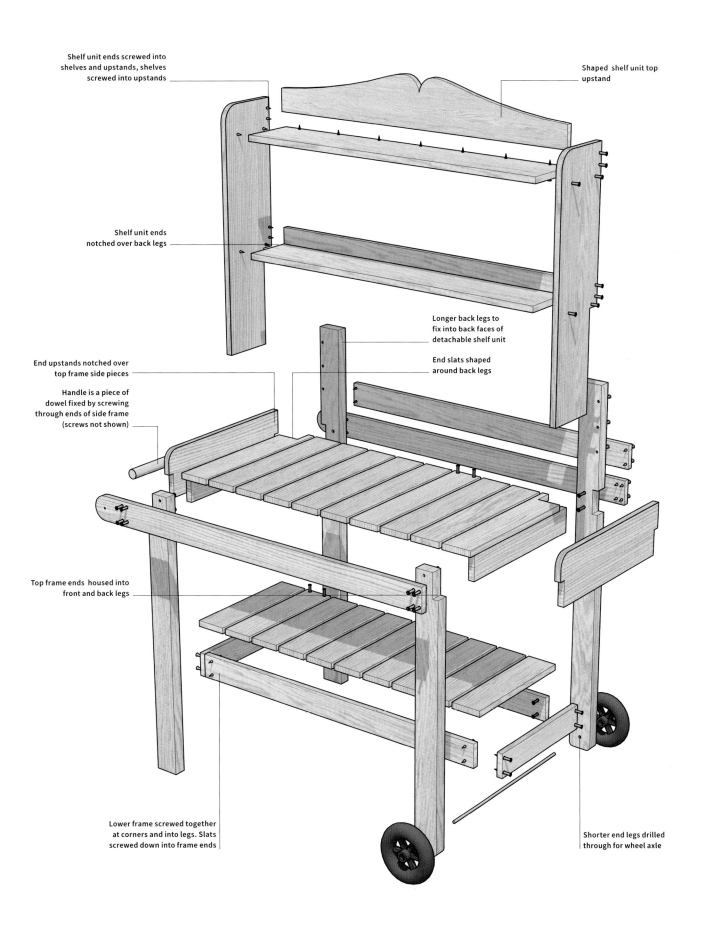

Shelf unit ends screwed into shelves and upstands, shelves screwed into upstands

Shaped shelf unit top upstand

Shelf unit ends notched over back legs

Longer back legs to fix into back faces of detachable shelf unit

End upstands notched over top frame side pieces

End slats shaped around back legs

Handle is a piece of dowel fixed by screwing through ends of side frame (screws not shown)

Top frame ends housed into front and back legs

Lower frame screwed together at corners and into legs. Slats screwed down into frame ends

Shorter end legs drilled through for wheel axle

GLOSSARY

arris A sharp edge formed where two surfaces meet.

chamfer To bevel the corner of a piece of wood at 45°.

crosscut To saw wood across the grain.

cross-dowel A fixing used for joining two pieces of wood, consisting of a metal cylinder with a threaded hole, inserted across the grain near the end of one component, and a bolt which is passed through the second component and into the cylinder. It is used to avoid driving a screw into the end grain, which would produce a weak joint.

cupped (of wood) Curved across the grain because of uneven moisture loss during seasoning.

datum A point, line or surface which is known to be accurate, from which subsequent measurements are made.

deepsawn (of a board) Sawn through its widest dimension, to produce boards the same width as the original piece, but thinner.

featherboard A safety device used with certain woodworking machines, fitted with comb-like, flexible teeth to hold the workpiece flat against the table or fence.

fence A straight guide on a tool such as a table saw or router table to keep the material a set parallel distance from the blade or cutter.

heartwood The harder wood produced near the centre of the tree trunk, as opposed to sapwood, formed in the outer layers.

jig Device used to control the location or motion of another tool.

kerf Make a narrow cut with a saw.

mitre box Apparatus to guide a saw to make mitre joints.

ogee An S-shaped curve.

outfeed The side of a power tool where the board exits.

pilot hole A hole slightly smaller than the thread diameter of a screw, which is drilled in a workpiece to prevent it from splitting.

quartersawn Sawn so that the growth rings in the timber are perpendicular to the surface; this minimizes subsequent warping or distortion of the wood.

resaw To reduce a sawn piece of wood to smaller pieces before making it into individual objects or components.

rip To saw wood along the grain.

rod A template – either literally a rod, or a wider board – on which the lengths of components and the positions of joints are marked for future reference.

roundover A rounded shape applied to the corner of a piece of wood to soften the edge.

sacrificial board An expendable piece of wood that is used to prevent damage to the workpiece, e.g. by placing it underneath a piece to be drilled so that any splintering which occurs damages only the sacrificial piece.

sanding bat A sanding aid consisting of a flat board covered with abrasive paper.

sanding through the grits (or grades) Sanding using progressively finer grades of abrasive.

sapwood The softer wood formed in the outer layers of the growing tree.

shake A split in wood, caused by trauma, internal stresses or unequal moisture loss.

shoot To plane the edge or end of a piece of wood, often while it is resting on a support called a shooting board.

snipe Rounding over of the ends of a board, caused by letting the plane tip at the beginning or end of its stroke.

spelching Splintering of the back edge of a workpiece during sawing or end-grain planing, caused by the pressure of the blade against the unsupported fibres.

through-and-through or **slabsawing** Sawing a log into parallel slices to minimize wastage.

tote The handle of certain tools, such as saws or planes.

waney-edged Incorporating part of the natural surface of the tree, often including the bark.

INDEX

To order a book, or to request a catalogue, contact:

GMC Publications Ltd

Castle Place, 166 High Street, Lewes, East Sussex

BN7 1XU, United Kingdom

Tel: +44 (0)1273 488005

www.gmcbooks.com